Psychiatry and the Humanities, Volume 8

Opening Texts:
Psychoanalysis and the Culture of the Child

Associate Editor
Christine Moustakis, M. Litt.

Assistant Editor
Gloria H. Parloff

Editorial Assistants
Carolyn Wheaton
Katherine S. Henry

Published under the auspices of the
Forum on Psychiatry and the Humanities
The Washington School of Psychiatry

Opening Texts

Psychoanalysis and the
Culture of the Child

Edited by
Joseph H. Smith, M.D.
William Kerrigan, Ph.D.

The Johns Hopkins University Press, 701 West 40th Street,
Baltimore, Maryland 21211
The Johns Hopkins Press Ltd., London

The paper in this book is acid-free and meets the
guidelines for permanence and durability of the
Committee on Production Guidelines for Book Longevity
of the Council on Library Resources.

Library of Congress Cataloging in Publication Data
Main entry under title:

Opening texts.

(Psychiatry and the humanities; v. 8)
Bibliography: p.
Includes index.
    1. Children's literature—History and criticism—Addresses, essays, lectures.
2. Children—Addresses, essays, lectures.   3. Psychoanalysis—Addresses,
essays, lectures.   I. Smith, Joseph H., 1927–   .   II. Kerrigan, William,
1943–   .   III. Series.
RC321.P943 vol. 8 [PN1009.A1] 616.89 s 84-43078
ISBN 0-8018-2680-2 (alk. paper) [809'.89282]

Contributors

Anne Scott MacLeod
Professor of Children's Literature, College of
Library and Information Services, University of
Maryland, College Park

Steven Marcus
Professor, Department of English, Columbia
University

Samuel Pickering, Jr.
Professor, Department of English, University of
Connecticut

Roger Sale
Professor of English, University of Washington

Maria Tatar
Professor of Germanic Languages and Literatures,
Harvard University

Nicholas Tucker
Faculty, Developmental Psychology, University of
Sussex, England

Jack Zipes
Professor of German and Comparative Literature,
University of Wisconsin—Milwaukee

Contents

Introduction

William Kerrigan

It opens traditionally enough with a bath of welcoming words and maybe a lullaby. But soon it takes contemporary form. Pink or blue; stuffed animals; a crib gym; music boxes; water toys; teething rings and pacifiers; jack-in-the-boxes; the great wardrobe of outgrown costumes, beginning perhaps with pants that snap open for easy changing and shirts like billboards to place on display hearts, flowers, rainbows, or comets; blocks; cloth books, coloring books, picture books, puzzle books, bedtime books, books; squawky telephones and tea sets; dolls and dollhouses; protean clay; their own stars in their own records, films, and TV shows; a proliferating clutter of icons drawn from the interlocking play worlds of corporate advertising, comic books, and other media, including children's literature; promotional gimmicks no longer limited to cereals and bubble gums, but growing along with the products themselves; their own food; concepts, such as "children's" or, in the play worlds, "otherworld" (Earth II, Middle Earth, Fourth Dimension, Subspace, Long Ago in a Galaxy Far Away); games to be played with adults or other children, in the house, on the sidewalk, in a field, on a screen, with cards, boards, dice, and spinners, or ropes, balls, and frisbees graded from Beginner to Professional; a succession of vehicles, from the first dump truck to the teen-age consummation of the automobile; a succession of weapons from the first plastic knife to the teen-age consummation of BB guns and martial-arts armament; elaborate donative rites on feasts and holidays; dances and parties, fairs and amusement parks, plays and parades, caverns and reconstructed dinosaurs; their own religious activities; athletics; lessons; camps; schools.

This formidable array of objects, rituals, and fictions that upbringers in the industrial West pass down to their young like a

ladder to adulthood, or like loose platonic essences whose instances
unfold (dump truck, wagon, tricycle, sled, scooter, bicycle) toward
mature stability (car) with apparently infinite room for expansion in
between, is a veritable second culture wrapped in the arms of culture
at large. Adults register their concern and alarm. If schooling is to the
culture of the child what work is to the culture of men and women,
then how educational is the small culture's extravagant investment in
recreation? What are the effects? Certain dismay rewards the alarmed,
for the little culture has proven as recalcitrant to fundamental change
as the parent culture. Growing up has become in significant ways an
autonomous process, mechanized, programmed. Adults, intellectuals
especially, tend to feel that they control their drift through culture,
and in the humanities intellectuals with this feeling now confront a
new generation of postmodernists emphasizing instead the play of
chance and the impotence of intention. The new feeling seems more
plausible when we look down from serious scholarship to the miniature logos in which our children are enmeshed.

The child's culture is a fairly recent invention, as we know in considerable detail from the work done on it, particularly its literature, in
recent decades. The present volume of our series is in part a tribute to
this new body of scholarship, which has opened a long-needed conversation. All but two of these papers focus on children's literature. It
may seem—and sometimes it is—an old-fashioned piety to single out
literature from the rest of the second culture as the element most
deserving of study, and then (as often happens) to cast it as hero or
culprit in the drama of this culture's evolution. For through the whole
bulk of the little culture, holding together its objects and activities,
are stories, a great weave of narrative beginning with the cradle that
must fall, and passing through family, national, world, and religious
history, fairy tales, fibs, rumors, cautionary examples, jokes, the facts
of life from myth or near myth to scrubbed science, television (that
story grinder), summer-camp ghost stories, the active-voice vacation
chronicles assigned in school, and so on. But there are reasons to assert
the primacy of literature, one of them being that through the fairy
tale, which is the primal form of children's literature, we gain clearest
access to the time when the second culture did not exist in material
form, that oral once-upon-a-time when the forest held wonders
enough, and there appears to have been, to the delight of this century's structuralists, only one essence—the great narrative invitation of
the fairy tale's otherworld, whose finite items were worked out (sometimes with systematic evasions, as Tatar argues here with respect to the
Brothers Grimm; see also Ellis, 1983) over the civilized world in boun-

tiful permutations. Today we have a mass of differentia, as codes have invaded every opening in the child's world. Our five-year-olds know perfectly well what distinguishes them from kids a year up or down the ladder. The ladder has infinitely more rungs; more essences unfold. Novelty, a plenitude of graduations, marks the second culture today. We rarely discover among its texts and artifacts the sense of completion, of realized combination and explored vision, evoked in the fairy tales.

A brief account of how those told stories became children's literature, and children's literature the flagship of children's culture, can begin (with an English bias) in the sixteenth century. English humanists, proud in their classical learning, scorned literature without the moral weight and stylistic decorum achieved in antiquity. The result was a division even in vernacular literature between popular and serious. Spenser's *Faerie Queen* provides the best example of how an old vernacular genre like romance, which even here combines easily with the folklore of elves and fairies, could not pass for High Renaissance Literature without becoming vigilantly aware of its own intellectual seriousness, yoking its narrative to the lessons of a university education. We find it in the history of literature side by side with unpretentious romances, chapbooks, ballads—texts aimed at those without education, which is to say, without Latin and the learning available in Latin. To be without education is to be, in certain senses, a child, and presumably children and adults mingled in the audience of popular literature. The next step was to separate them by targeting children. By the end of the seventeenth century, collections of fairy tales intended for children had been published in France. But in England the early humanist disdain for mere story joined with the new Protestant demand for education as a guided route to moral and social respectability, a discipline for unruly imagination, to produce in the eighteenth century a new industry, as publishers such as Boreman and Newbery issued Lockean alternatives to romance and fairy tale (Pickering, 1981; and in this volume). By and large this literature remained faithful, with some new utilitarian angles, to the venerable idea that childhood was fundamentally a state of privation. Children were not yet citizens, not yet responsible or rightly self-interested, not yet rational.

We know that Wordsworth's half-creating perceiver opposed the emptied ego of British empiricism. When his poetry about childhood is set against the children's literature inspired by Locke, suggestive inversions appear. In Wordsworth the adult repeatedly encounters deprivation, and schools it by reanimating the brimming fullness of childhood. The child, best philosopher, is the inward educator who throughout life must instruct the wayward adult. He is also the benefactor or patron, since the cash of imagination can only be drawn from a trust fund deposited in early memories.

Imagination in Western dualism had been the liminal faculty between perception and reason, body and mind, object and subject—literally so in the picture of brain physiology that dominated medicine from Galen through the Renaissance. Normally it was consigned to the subordinate side of the hierarchy as the slave of things, charged with recombining pieces of perception. Reason was the one, singular and constant, while imagination amplified variety, appearance, and error. Now and then, as in Neoplatonism, reason claimed imagination as the house organ of *mens,* imprinter of intuitive vision. The history of the new culture played out in pragmatic ways these austere philosophical maneuvers. By curbing romance with didactic realism, the Lockean tradition of children's literature sought to make imagination as resolute, fixed, and routed as reason itself. In Wordsworth, however, reason is not the sweet of adulthood, but its deprivation. Nor is reason singular. As Steven Marcus intimates in the Weigert lecture that opens this book, his encounters with children in poems such as "We Are Seven" and "Anecdote for Fathers" split reason. The mind's child, imagination, when judged by grown-up philosophical reason, seemed to be fracturing rational solidity. Now Wordsworth, beholding reason from the imagination of the child, implies that there are indeed variant rationalities—two ways of calculating, two ways of knowing what you think.

"A child is psychologically a different object from an adult" (Freud, *S.E.* 22:148). Psychoanalysis is the science of the new culture. "Children," Freud announced in 1925, "have become the main subjects of psycho-analytic research and have thus replaced in importance the neurotics on whom its studies began" (*S.E.* 19:273). The insights of poets like Wordsworth are now laid bare in serious prose, for psychoanalysis "has been obliged to derive the mental life of adults from that of children, and has had to take seriously the old saying that the child is father to the man" (*S.E.* 13:183). There are in fact two principles of mental functioning, a primary and a secondary process. There is in fact a prototypical rationality that knows no "no," no contradiction, no loss or death. The fateful child is in fact the father and mother of adults, whose tasks they obediently continue to perform.

But Freud was interestingly ambivalent about the proper relationship between psychoanalysis and the new culture. He analyzed its games, showing how much real psychic work might be getting done in

dandling a spool from a string. He analyzed folktales and super-
stitions. He sometimes termed therapy itself a *Nacherziehung*, or
"belated upbringing": "Education is a prophylaxis, which is intended to obviate both outcomes—neurosis and perversion alike;
psychotherapy seeks to undo the less stable of the two outcomes and
to institute a kind of after-education [*Nacherziehung*]" (*S.E.* 12:330).
Thus Freud assures us that he himself would have told Little Hans the
straight story of penis, vagina, and impregnation had he been the
boy's father (*S.E.* 10:145), and as analyst or belated upbringer, that is
more or less what he actually does. Though wary of endorsing social
reform with the authority of psychoanalysis, Freud made exceptions in
the case of education. Here, for example, we find him uncharacteristi-
cally testy in writing of the "mystery-making" obfuscations that parents and educators throw up before the sexual curiosity of children:
"To be sure, if it is the purpose of educators to stifle the child's power
of independent thought as early as possible, in favour of the 'goodness' which they think so much of, they cannot set about this better
than by deceiving him in sexual matters and intimidating him in
matters of religion" (*S.E.* 9:136–37). This is one of the most judgmental sentences in all of Freud. At the end of his open letter on
sexual enlightenment, he gives way to a familiar gesture of social
reformers, who, exasperated at the errors mired in this stubborn
world, counter their despair with the utopian vision of cleansing an
entire generation by seizing power in the new culture. It is Freud's
psychoanalytic *Aufklärung:* "Here, once again, we see the unwisdom
of sewing a single silk patch on to a tattered coat—the impossibility of
carrying out an isolated reform without altering the foundations of
the whole system" (p. 139).

Yet, looking beyond this zeal, a barrier has been left intact between
psychoanalysis and the culture of the child. Freud has simply recommended the truth, and the truth, it should be noted, upon the child's
request. There may be psychoanalytic reasons for answering a question frankly, but the true answer is not itself "psychoanalytic." Freud
grew reluctant at the thought of introducing the actual content of
psychoanalytic *Nacherziehung* into *Erziehung* proper. While he several times recommended that educators should be analyzed (*S.E.* 12;
19:274; 22:150), he maintained that "the work of education is something *sui generis:* it is not to be confused with psycho-analytic influence and cannot be replaced by it" (*S.E.* 19:274). Why did Freud
resist the temptation to become didactic, invading the new culture he
knew so much about with his own brand of enlightenment? What, for
instance, is wrong—and I think it is wrong, and that Freud also
thought so—about explaining to an anxious child the castration com-

plex? One answer is that we would be interfering in a highly rational manner with an instinctual process that would simply go its own way, making use of whatever obstacles we put on its path. Another answer lies in Freud's insistence that upbringing is *sui generis*. He wisely suspected that to mingle upbringing with psychoanalysis was to risk the contamination of both enterprises on a grand scale. As we in this Freudian age know from our public debates, if not from the quarrels in our marriages, psychoanalysis often comes to life with aggressive rather than therapeutic intent. I hope it will not seem sour of me to emphasize, in these opening remarks, that almost everything in the new culture of the child has, or can have, a hostile cast.

In the earliest records of European lullabies Tucker finds two prominent stances—an exuberant maternal love that promises the moon to a restless infant, and a savage maternal rage that threatens just as lavishly. Throughout children's literature mature versions of these postures alternate and combine. There are fulfilled wishes, happy endings, huge rewards; there are also fearsome enemies, hard cautions, pessimistic discouragements. The two may fuse. Wish fulfillment can be so unchecked that the story seems to be laying a trap, setting up a fall for its credulous audience. As Zipes notes in this book, many adults have felt that life's disappointments crystallize about the failed covenants of their first literature—no solvable riddle, no magic ring, and no Prince Charming. And the sort of literature that takes pride in its delivery of corrective "realism" may readily lapse into subtle forms of punishment, as MacLeod suggests in her essay on recent teen-age fiction. The dialectic of utilitarianism and amusement loosed in Dickens's *Hard Times* is not so easy to resolve. We have no trouble observing the anti-fun aggression in some of the Lockean books of the eighteenth century. But this aggression, because it is inevitable, reroots itself in every stage of the new culture, including the Romantic idealization of the child. In the very same poems that convey his discovery of the alien mind of the child, Wordsworth also manifests his adult desire to violate and abolish this difference— to end childhood. The idiotic girl of "We Are Seven" must learn to add it right, and the dummy of "Anecdote for Fathers" must learn to talk like an adult, supplying reasons for his feelings. "Even in many books which idealize children," Sale has contended, "the implicit rhetoric insists it is better to be an adult, and thereby be able to do this idealizing, than it is to be a child, who doesn't know any better than not to know that his or hers is the ideal time of life" (1978, pp. 64–65).

At the swimming pool I use in the summertime a lane has been roped off for exercise. I feel I see something when, in the long afternoons, health-minded adults one after another count out their laps with disciplined strokes, while next to them heedless young people splash and frolic. No wonder we are so concerned with making lappers of them! Our aggression toward children runs deep. Generations envy each other, inevitably. Time has an ominous swell: as one grows up another passes away. The young watch themselves come into their strength and sexual power while the parental generation gradually loses strength and sexual power. The aging watch the same process. And to everyone watching, it may appear as if the young flourish literally on the lost energies of the older generation—that a siphon, as it were, drains vitality from one generation to pour it on another.

In the seventeenth century, on the threshold of children's culture, Bishop King began a conventional panegyric welcoming the son of Charles I, but soon swerved into disturbing and universal truth:

> For howere Children, unto those that look
> Their Pedigree in God's, not the Church book,
> Fair pledges are of that eternitie
> Which Christians possess not till they die;
> Yet they appear view'd in that perspective
> Through which we look on men long since alive,
> Like succours in a Camp, sent to make good
> Their place that last upon the watches stood.
> So that in age, or fate, each following birth
> Doth set the Parent so much neerer earth:
> And by this Grammar we our heirs may call
> The smiling Prefact to our funerall.
> . . . .
> But here with fate we dally, and in this
> Stern Destiny mocks and controules our wish;
> Informing us, if fathers should remain
> For ever here, children were born in vain; . . . [King, pp. 38–39]

Yet wishes are precisely that brood of our brainchildren who do not submit to fate. As the bourgeois hero of Updike's *Rabbit Is Rich* holds in his arms for the first time, and with a degree of triumph, his first grandchild, he is inevitably compelled to reflect, "Another nail in his coffin. His " (1982, p. 437). This changing of the guards, this slow crowding out, may look more like thievery than orderly transition. The young may feel that the goods of life are being hoarded by the parental generation, and must therefore be stolen. For their part, the old guard may resent youthful vitality, and impose strictures on it. Once the new culture arrives, and former children who have suffered the disillusionments of growing up—and now experience the disillusionments of being crowded out—begin to hand down in literature the apple of knowledge, they may have some stake in poisoning it.

The stepmother queen of "Snow White" lives in every adult: so long as the young are busy, chaste, and disillusioned, they are not really enjoying the daily perfecting of their triumph; so long as they are coddled, fooled, and set up, they are dependent on us, and without us head for sure disappointment. The new culture of the child materializes the siphon that takes from the passing away and gives to the growing up. Its vital liquors are not an unmixed blessing.

But at its most sublime, good wishes for children merge with hostile suspicion of their brief paradise to engender an authentic literature of hope, which may be defined psychoanalytically as a wish that has internalized the possibility of its failure (Kerrigan, 1983, p. 297). From the best of their culture children may learn both to mourn, shedding illusion, and to want, shedding despair. Hope is the dominant tone of children's literature, and we are surely right to become alarmed when we encounter hopelessness in the new culture. "The doctor," Freud wrote, in his most telling distinction between *Erziehung* and psychoanalytic *Nacherziehung,* "has as a rule to deal with psychical structures which have already become rigid and he will find in the patient's established individuality a limit to his own achievement but at the same time a guarantee of the patient's capacity to stand alone. The educator, however, works upon material which is plastic and open to every impression" (*S.E.* 12:331). The child, who presents his caretakers with no "limit," is not yet a patient, and may hope never to become a patient.

About this "material which is plastic and open to every impression"—this openness or futurity or hopefulness that is for Freud the essence of the child, and the main reason why psychoanalysis must not conceive of itself as an instrument of education belonging to the culture of the child—we may seek instruction in the culture at large. There appeared, concurrently with the evolution of the second culture, a new way of measuring the value of an adult life. All things are best measured in extremity, before the specter of their loss, and in literature it is tragedy that holds before us a mirror of squandered greatness. Tragedy, the least assimilated of the major genres into the miniature literature of the child, enables us to appreciate what the task of that literature should be.

The heroes of Shakespeare know nothing of the new culture. In the final act, having borne their tragedies, they remember their mature triumphs, the noons of noble achievement: the misery of tragic destiny is measured by reference to their deeds of greatness. But in the Romantic period, with the flowering of the new culture, we confront a new form of tragic pathos. Blake's Thel, with her infant desire to nourish and mother, listens in horror to the repressed and disillusioned voice of the dead virgin in her own grave. The juxtaposition of innocent hope with experienced despair, not mature greatness with its fallen state, measures the value of life. Pathos takes this shape at the conclusion of Wordsworth's "Ruth":

> I, too, have passed her on the hills
> Setting her little water-mills
> By spouts and fountains wild—
> Such small machinery as she turned
> Ere she had wept, ere she had mourned,
> A young and happy child!

The old beggarwoman handles her trinkets as once, "Ere she had wept, ere she had mourned," she turned her toys. That is what tragedy has come to mean: an aperture closed over the infinite hopes of a child. Another and more complex example occurs in *Wuthering Heights*, when Lockwood visits the Grange and is assigned the room that once belonged to Cathy:

> The ledge, where I placed my candle, had a few mildewed books in one corner; and it was covered with writing scratched on the paint. This writing, however, was nothing but a name repeated in all kinds of characters, large and small—*Catherine Earnshaw:* here and there varied to *Catherine Heathcliff,* and then again to *Catherine Linton.* [Brontë, 1965, p. 61]

The scratched names commemorate that "plastic" time "open to every impression" when several lives are possible, and a young girl thinks of marrying him or him. Fate, though, has one answer. Cathy became Catherine Linton. Soon her ghost appears to Lockwood as "a child's face looking through the window" of her old room. Here again pathos arises from the "child's face" in the grave of unanswered hope. The new tragic pathos also emerges in one of the great moments in cinema. How to measure the bloated loneliness of Kane in Xanadu? We saw it for a moment in an early frame, and there it is again, the sled on the fire: Rosebud.

Insofar as children's literature guides hope, it of course presupposes values. We may even call it ideological. But the moral hope in children's culture need not be a matter of teaching rules and precepts, and the virtue of obeying them. In *After Virtue* Alasdair MacIntyre argues that our philosophers of ethics have for some centuries been pursuing the blatant folly of trying to deduce moral formulae, then anchor them in some necessitating ground. Our entire conception of virtue descends from communities that never doubted for a moment the validity of their ways. Virtues in the Greek polis were learned from stories about the heroes of another age:

> If a human life is understood as a progress through harms and dangers, moral and physical, which someone may encounter and overcome in better and worse ways and with a greater or lesser measure of success, the virtues will find their place as those qualities the possession and exercise of which generally tend to success in this enterprise and the vices likewise as qualities which likewise tend to failure. Each human life will then embody a story whose shape and form will depend upon what is counted as a harm and danger and upon how success and failure, progress and its opposite, are understood and evaluated. To answer these questions will also explicitly and implicitly be to answer the question as to what the virtues and vices are. The answer to this linked set of questions given by the poets of heroic society is not the same as that given by Sophocles; but the link is the same in both, and it reveals how belief in the virtues being of a certain kind and belief in human life exhibiting a certain narrative order are internally connected. [1981, p. 135]

If there can be, for readers so distant from ancient Athens, something compelling about this argument, I suspect it is because our early stories, whatever they may have intended, served us in this fashion. We hoped. The future opened. We knew what would be wonderful, what would be dire. Virtue was better as example than as rule. In the stories were people or animal-people of all ages, but mostly or centrally the young, leaving home, learning their true friends and enemies, wanting something, figuring out the rules, trying to win. Everything that happens in a story, because it does happen in a story, receives the honor of being remembered: however quietly, they taught us of glory. One difference between the stories of Athens and the stories of today is that another culture awaits our children, in which these early nobilities will suffer diminishment, and they will probably have to scratch about for rules and directions, learning from experience how tragically arbitrary the whole business of being virtuous can look these days. Ethnic and class traditions orient the culture of the child, and if that culture is to be hopeful, a further measure of insularity is necessary. Everyone has been prepared for something less than the entirety of adult experience. Most children pay a toll in chagrin as they move from their first culture to what Sale terms in the memoir that closes this volume "all that I was ignorant of, all that had been kept from me by people and circumstance." But we cannot hear often enough that the worst tragedy is to have no hope at all. Generations must be allowed to find their own disillusionment, as (laying our aggressions at the doorstep of fate, where they belong) they surely will. The world keeps spinning down, a little more smudged every day. The patients keep coming.

I have an anecdote for fathers and mothers. One day as I was leaving for work, feeling very sorry for myself over some recent setbacks, my five-year-old son followed me to the car, and for no reason at all, smiled at me. Rosebud. He was so unaccountably radiant that I, not so unaccountably, began to cry, struck by a sudden conviction that nothing in life—not the love of beautiful women, not the joy of accomplishment and success—would prove answerable to such a smile unless it were having helped to engender one. Both of us can also be real bastards. We read books together.

References

Brontë, Emily. *Wuthering Heights*. New York: Penguin, 1965.

Ellis, John. *One Fairy Tale Too Many: The Brothers Grimm and Their Tales*. Chicago: University of Chicago Press, 1983.

Freud, Sigmund. *The Standard Edition of the Complete Psychological Works*. Edited and translated by James Strachey. London: Hogarth, 1953–74:

"The Sexual Enlightenment of Children" (1907), vol. 9.

Analysis of a Phobia in a Five-Year-Old Boy (1909), vol. 10.

"Introduction to Pfister's *The Psycho-analytic Method*" (1913a), vol. 12.

"The Claims of Psycho-analysis to Scientific Interest" (1913b), vol. 13.

"Preface to Aichhorn's *Wayward Youth*" (1925), vol. 19.

New Introductory Lectures (1933), vol. 22.

Kerrigan, William. *The Sacred Complex: On the Psychogenesis of Paradise Lost*. Cambridge, Mass.: Harvard University Press, 1983.

King, Henry. *The Poems of Bishop Henry King*. Edited by James Baker. Denver: Swallow, 1960.

MacIntyre, Alasdair. *After Virtue*. Notre Dame, Ind.: University of Notre Dame Press, 1981.

Pickering, Samuel. *John Locke and Children's Books in Eighteenth-Century England*. Knoxville: University of Tennessee Press, 1981.

Sale, Roger. *Fairy Tales and After: From Snow White to E. B. White*. Cambridge, Mass.: Harvard University Press, 1978.

Updike, John. *Rabbit Is Rich*. New York: Ballantine, 1982.

Psychiatry and the Humanities, Volume 8

Opening Texts:
Psychoanalysis and the Culture of the Child

1   Some Representations of Childhood in Wordsworth's Poetry

Steven Marcus

As J. H. Plumb has written, in an article of 1975 called "The New World of Children in Eighteenth-Century England" that has become something of a classic, the "history of children remains obscure." Though some pioneering work had been done before Plumb's essay, and more systematic attention has been focused upon the subject since, the field of inquiry still remains, if I may say so, in its state of infancy. One thing seems fairly certain, however; as Plumb remarks toward the end of his study, "wherever we turn in the world of children [in eighteenth-century England]—clothes, pets, toys, education, sport, music and art, their world was richer, more varied, more intellectually and emotionally exciting than it had been in earlier generations."

An inevitable concomitant of this group of changes was the increasing intellectual and cultural attention being trained upon childhood; and in the realm of literature from the latter part of the period, three figures stand out today as having made definitive contributions to the new realization or understanding of what children were—I refer, of course, to Rousseau, Blake, and Wordsworth. In what follows, I want to direct our notice toward certain representations of childhood in some relatively early poems by Wordsworth, and I want to do so in the light they cast prospectively forward toward what would be formulated one hundred years later as psychoanalytic theory and clinical observation; reciprocally, I should like to use the knowledge we have acquired from the psychoanalytic discipline to help us recognize certain things that happen in these poems.

The first poem I chose was included in the original edition of *Lyrical Ballads* (1798); it is called "We Are Seven," and I have a prejudice of belief that almost anyone who has attained some degree of higher

1

literacy in English has probably read it. It is a typical lyrical ballad in the effort it makes toward directness, plainness, and factuality in its diction, in the conversational unevenness of its meter, and in the artfully contrived, naïve tone of the traditional balladeer that Wordsworth is able to work about with considerable adroitness. The poem begins with disarming simplicity, announcing its theme at once in its first stanzaic utterance:

> A simple Child,
> That lightly draws its breath,
> And feels its life in every limb,
> What should it know of death?

Children cannot understand what death is or means; the idea must have been a commonplace even then—Rousseau mentions it in *Emile*—but no one, to my knowledge, had ever regarded it in just the way that Wordsworth did in this early poem. In his Preface to the 1800 edition of *Lyrical Ballads,* Wordsworth refers to this poem in a particular context. He is asserting, in the face of adverse critics, that each of these poems "has a purpose." In this connection, he calls the poems in question "short essays," using the term in a sense that he derives, I believe, from Montaigne, as trials or enquiries into experience; and of "We Are Seven," he remarks that his purpose was to show "the perplexity and obscurity which in childhood attend our notion of death, or rather our utter inability to admit that notion."

The poem continues in its second stanza:

> I met a little cottage Girl:
> She was eight years old, she said . . .

Nothing could be more "natural" than this report of a chance encounter (that apparently took place, incidentally, five years before the composition of the poem). What is implied is that the grown young man has asked one of the few conventional questions that an adult (or anyone else for that matter) addresses to a child on a first meeting and gets a direct answer to his question; but what is also introduced with this plain factual response is an anticipation of the rather elaborate numbers game that the rest of the poem will expand upon. And the poem almost immediately begins on that expansion.

> "Sisters and brothers, little Maid,
> How many may you be?"
> "How many? Seven in all," she said,
> And wondering looked at me.

This second, overt question is as traditional, conventional, and "natural" as the first implied enquiry; and the response offered by the girl is as straightforward as her first answer was. But the first interpretative node, or matrix of sudden impaction or increased density of meaning, comes about in the word "wondering." Our moving, reading eyes are momentarily stopped by it. Why is she wondering at this question? What is there in it that causes her to cock a look of wonderment, or surprise, or reciprocal interrogation, back at the young poet? Reflection makes it apparent, I think, that she believes the question to be otiose or superfluous and therefore slightly foolish. The implied content of that look, as I read it, is, "Don't you know?" or "Everyone knows, so why are you asking?" One part of the child's consciousness regards the entire world as coterminous with her family; in this context—though not in others—there are no strangers in the world, and so the question is silly and redundant. But at the same moment, as we recognize part of the meaning of that look of counterinterrogation, there begins to open up in us the presentiment that this is not simply a dialogue between a mature young man and a girl of eight, but that two different realms of being are confronting one another, two realms that are related by their difference, disconnection, and disparity as much as they are by the common English language that both connects and, paradoxically, separates them in their shared incommensurability of reference.

There then follows the third and climactic permutation of the numbers game that these two interlocutors are unconsciously playing.

"And where are they? I pray you tell."
She answered, "Seven are we;
And two of us by Conway dwell,
And two are gone to sea.

"Two of us in the church-yard lie,
My sister and my brother;
And, in the church-yard cottage, I
Dwell near them with my mother."

"You say that two at Conway dwell,
And two are gone to sea,
Yet you are seven! I pray you tell,
Sweet Maid, how this may be."

They have locked horns and will not unlock them again until their mutual parting at the end of the poem. For they enter now upon a purposeless argument, which can come to no conclusion in the terms that the two protagonists perforce employ. It is unmistakably clear that the notion of death is fundamentally only a word for this little girl, and that it means in part only that her two dead siblings have "gone away," just as the other four have who are not at present living with her and her mother. They have "gone away," but in another sense they are "still here." And at his point the reader begins to realize that the poem might just as well have been called—as I think someone did once call it—"The Arithmetic Lesson"; that the lesson that has to be learned is that seven minus two can equal seven; and that the person who has to learn this lesson is the young poet and not the little girl. What he has to learn is that for her, for a child in her situation, seven minus two equals seven is as real, as rational, and as self-evident as the alternative form of that equation, which she will undoubtedly discover later when she learns to apply the arithmetic of abstract numbers that we all have to be acculturated to, to her own intimate experience. Subtraction is a cruel lesson.

But the poet does not discern this at once, and he proceeds to argue with the little girl in order to convince her of the correspondence of his arithmetic to the real world. He cannot do so, but in the course of her responses to him, we learn more about her child's sense of life and death.

> "Their graves are green, they may be seen,"
> The little Maid replied,
> "Twelve steps or more from my mother's door,
> And they are side by side.
>
> "My stockings there I often knit,
> My kerchief there I hem;
> And there upon the ground I sit,
> And sing a song to them."

Her relation to death is, in an interesting way, analogous to the relation represented by Wordsworth in his spectacularly old figures, such as the Old Cumberland Beggar, or the anonymous ancient creature in "Animal Tranquillity and Decay." These figures have passed into such extreme old age and feebleness that they are at the very edge of sentience, are no longer conscious, it seems, of existence or death, or of the difference between them, and represent fundamental or irreducible humanity, in the sense that any further alteration of them would represent a transfiguration of the organic into something like the inorganic. The little girl exists toward the opposite, farther (or nearer) end of this spectrum. She has not yet fully experienced in consciousness the separation that death represents. She has not yet undergone sufficiently the kind of differentiation of herself from other objects of love that makes grief and mourning consciously accessible to her; and, indeed, she does not apparently feel sorrow for her dead brother and sister; in their graves they still remain a living part of her community, just as in village churchyards in Europe, the dead are regarded as still belonging to the community of the living. The poem ends in irony.

> "But they are dead; those two are dead!
> Their spirits are in heaven!"
> 'Twas throwing words away; for still
> The little Maid would have her will,
> And said, "Nay, we are seven!"

"Throwing words away" might be an ironically oblique yet apt means of describing the action of this poem, for one of its insights surely is that the poet and the young girl have different relations to words and language and therefore to the real world that both inhabit in such different ways. And of course there is in addition the irony of who is doing the "will"-ing in this poem, the insistent, pedagogical young poet, or the assured, unshakable, and equally insistent little girl.

Perhaps the best final comment that I can bring to bear upon this little poem, or "essay," was written about one hundred years later. In Chapter 5 of *The Interpretation of Dreams*, Freud writes:

> The fear of death has no meaning to a child; hence it is that he will play with the dreadful word and use it as a threat against a playmate: "If you do that again, you'll die, like Franz!" Meanwhile the poor mother gives a shudder and remembers, perhaps, that the greater half of the human race fail to survive their childhood years. It was actually possible for a child, who was over eight years old at the time, coming home from a visit to the Natural History Museum, to say to his mother: "I'm so fond of you, Mummy: when you die I'll have you stuffed and I'll keep you in this room, so that I can see you *all* the time." So little resemblance is there between a child's idea of being dead and our own!
>
> To children, who, moreover, are spared the sight of the scenes of suffering which precede death, being "dead" means approximately the same as being "gone." . . . A child makes no distinction as to how this absence is brought about: whether it is due to a journey, to a dismissal, to an estrangement, or to death. [*S.E.* 4:254–55]

And in 1909, Freud added another illustration in a footnote: "I was astonished," he writes, "to hear a highly intelligent boy of ten remark after the sudden death of his father: 'I know father's dead, but what I can't understand is why he doesn't come home to supper.'" Freud is making these observations in a fairly accented note of personal discovery; and I think it pertinent to add that this same note characterizes the general tone of Wordsworth's earlier traversal of the same ground.

The second poem I should like to discuss is the companion piece to "We Are Seven." "Anecdote for Fathers" is also animated by the covert suggestion that in the course of it—and the experience it is rehearsing—the poet is making some kind of new or hitherto unarticulated discovery about human experience. But it isn't evident that he is fully mindful what the discovery is. This less than complete illumination of what he is dramatizing is in part suggested by the two subtitles Wordsworth gave to this poem. The first subtitle was, "Shewing How The Art of Lying May Be Taught." The second, which replaced the first in 1845, was in Latin: "*Retine vim istam, falsa enim dicam, si coges.*" This is taken from Eusebius, *Preparatio Evengelica* 6.5, and is itself a translation from the Greek of Porphyry, and may be rendered into English as, "Restrain that force of yours, for I shall tell lies if you drive me to it." Whether in the ironic English original, or in the learned classical replacement, it should be evident to the careful reader of this poem that the poet doesn't entirely grasp what he is doing in this poem, for it is also about a good deal more than lying.

The poem's opening stanza contains a piece of dramatically useful poetic license:

> I have a boy of five years old;
> His face is fair and fresh to see;
> His limbs are cast in beauty's mould
> And dearly he loves me.

The boy in the poem was not Wordsworth's son; Wordsworth was not yet married (although he had an illegitimate daughter living in France). The boy was the illegitimate son of Wordsworth's friend Basil Montagu, and Wordsworth and his sister Dorothy had been caring for him, according to Wordsworth, for some "two or three years." There is no reason, therefore, to doubt the intimacy of their relation or the boy's love for his surrogate father that is asserted in the fourth line. That intimacy and love are reinforced in the second stanza.

> One morn we strolled on our dry walk,
> Our quiet home all full in view,
> And held such intermitted talk
> As we are wont to do.

The morning walk, it is implied, is customary or habitual, as is their "intermitted talk." The conversation, in other words, is relaxed, spontaneous, and unforced—they are used to one another, at ease with each other, at ease in their mutuality and affection.

The poet then turns to himself, and the next four stanzas consist of an exposition and examination of his current state of mind.

> My thoughts on former pleasures ran;
> I thought of Kilve's delightful shore,
> Our pleasant home when spring began,
> A long, long year before.
>
> A day it was when I could bear
> Some fond regrets to entertain;
> With so much happiness to spare,
> I could not feel a pain.
>
> The green earth echoed to the feet
> Of lambs that bounded through the glade,
> From shade to sunshine, and as fleet
> From sunshine back to shade.
>
> Birds warbled round me—and each trace
> Of inward sadness had its charm;
> Kilve, thought I, was a favored place,
> And so is Liswyn farm.

As he reflects on the pleasure he feels in the spring morning, his thoughts naturally revert to the similar pleasures he had experienced at a different place—Kilve, a village on the Bristol Channel—where they had lived a year before. But this year is also, for him, "a long, long year"; that is to say, much has occurred during that time, not all of it necessarily pleasant; and, even more, the poet, a grown man, is acutely aware of the passage of time—time for him is a terribly palpable reality.

Still, it is such a pleasant day, he goes on, that he can entertain some "fond regrets." He is using the word "fond" here in its older acceptation as "foolish"; what can be more foolish than to regret the inevitable and irremissive passage of time? Even so, in his current state of intense happiness and creativity, he can allow himself to be pulled both ways, to indulge or cosset himself in both ambivalence and contradiction—for if he feels regret, then how can he assert at the same time that he feels no pain? And these flickerings back and forth of opposed or contradictory emotions are metaphorically rerepresented in the lambs that bound back and forth between sunshine and shade. Moreover, in the fourth of these stanzas of self-examination, he elaborates further upon this ambivalence. As he thinks of the two pleasant places, the Kilve of a year ago, and the Liswyn farm of the dramatic present, he recognizes that "each trace of inward sadness had its charm." He is managing to extract a genuine degree of pleasure from the common experience of nostalgia; he is both regretting the irretrievable past and at the same moment recognizing and giving in to the inevitable. Such complexities of feeling about the irreversibility of time and our mortal existence within it are exemplary of us as grown people, as is our unsettled and uneasy set of emotions whenever we self-consciously examine this group of circumstances and attitudes.

It is both within and out of this condition of present pleasure and happiness with its undercurrent consciousness of the passage of time, admixed with an awareness of the futility of the emotion of regret, that the poet next acts. As he and his five-year-old companion and ward talk, he begins to question the boy "in very idleness." He is using "idleness" primarily, again, in the older sense of pointlessness or fatuity, of being without immediate or perceptible aim or purpose.

> "Now tell me, had you rather be,"
> I said, and took him by the arm,
> "On Kilve's smooth shore, by the green sea,
> Or here at Liswyn farm?"

This seems to be an innocent enough piece of chat, although there is something slightly ominous in his taking the boy by the arm at exactly this juncture. And we understand as well what he is doing; it is a common, familiar, and usually harmless device. He is momentarily relieving himself of a minor inner conflict by projecting his opposed and unreconciled feelings outward in the form of the question he puts to the boy. The boy, however, is not troubled by any of this behavior, and his reply is simple and unalloyed, though almost nothing that follows from that reply retains these qualities:

> In careless mood he looked at me,
> While still I held him by the arm,
> And said, "At Kilve I'd rather be
> Than here at Liswyn farm."

> "Now little Edward, say why so:
> My little Edward tell me why."

poem, too, like "We Are Seven," has about it the sense or aura that something new about experience is being disclosed in the course of its creation.

The third of the poems that I should like to discuss strikes something of a contrast to the first two. It is about an experience recollected by Wordsworth from his own childhood. It was, he later testified, originally intended to be part of *The Prelude,* the poem on his own life, on which he spent so much of that life, but he apparently never found an appropriate place for it in the unique narrative-discursive structure of that poem. In any event, he published it separately in 1800. The poem begins *in medias res,* indeed in the middle of a line:

> It seems a day
> (I speak of one from many singled out)
> One of those heavenly days that cannot die;
> When in the eagerness of boyish hope,
> I left our cottage-threshold, sallying forth
> With a huge wallet o'er my shoulder slung,
> A nutting-crook in hand; and turned my steps
> Tow'rd some far-distant wood, a Figure quaint,
> Tricked out in proud disguise of cast-off weeds
> Which for that service had been husbanded,
> By exhortation of my frugal Dame—
> Motley accoutrement, of power to smile
> At thorns, and brakes, and brambles—and, in truth,
> More ragged than need was!

The splendid opening lines contain an almost certainly deliberate ambiguity: does the "one" referred to apply to the day itself or to the young personage, the subject of the poem, the protopoet? I believe that the answer has to be "both." But there is nothing ambiguous about the day itself. It was one of those days that Wordsworth referred to as "spots of time"; we have all had experiences and recollections of experiences that bear upon his conception of this subject. He is talking about certain special moments from our usually early pasts that have the power of resisting the normal workings of erosion or wearing away, condensation, and affective deinvestment that ordinary memory regularly performs in us. These experiences, whether they be traumatically frightening, or ecstatic and transcendent, resist such processes, and may recur to us unbidden, and with all the freshness and impressiveness of their original occurrence at almost any time in later life. For Wordsworth, they constituted a considerable part of the experiential capital that he would draw upon during his poetic career.

Yet we must note that this special, intensified experience is deeply set in and rises out of a common and ordinary event or activity. Like other country boys of his time, young Wordsworth was accustomed to go out into the woods in the autumn to gather nuts: he was, he remarked in a later note, "an impassioned nutter." And in this poem, full with the "eagerness of boyish hope," he is setting forth on a familiar yet exciting adventure. This sense of adventure is compounded by how he is gotten up: his equipment consists of a "huge wallet" and a nutting-crook for pulling and tugging at tree branches and dislodging the hazelnuts on them; but he is also dressed in "cast-off weeds," possibly hand-me-downs, partly worn-out pieces of dress that might have once belonged to other or older members of the household and that were of especial use for rough wear in the woods. These in their heterogeneity and incongruity make a "motley accoutrement," and he imagines himself in that past as a "Figure quaint." And yet at the same time he remembers himself as being "Tricked out in proud disguise"—he is proud of being disguised, is full of the momentary self that he imagines himself to be. It is not difficult for us to recognize what is going on here. The boy is in disguise; he is playing at being someone else or other than he is. And if we ask why children habitually love to put on costumes, to wear the old clothes of their parents or elder siblings, to put on an old black hat and cry, "I'm Captain Hook," or a sheet or torn tablecloth and shout out "Batman" or "Superman," we do not have to search far to find a sufficiency of answers. These costumes and disguises are deep parts of play, in particular those kinds of play in which, for a suspended moment or stretch of privileged time, the child experiences a sense of moral liberation, or release from habitual constraints. It represents an opportunity for him or her to exercise freedom or power not normally within the child's permissible range of behavior. This is why such scenes or experiences almost always contain dramatic enactments of aggression—"zap; you're dead," or "off with his head," or "take his money, and tie him up." They are necessary moments of our education in life, and they are what the poem is in considerable measure about, as Wordsworth, without pause, continues:

O'er pathless rocks,
Through beds of matted fern, and tangled thickets,
Forcing my way, I came to one dear nook
Unvisited, where not a broken bough
Drooped with its withered leaves, ungracious sign
Of devastation; but the hazels rose
Tall and erect, with tempting clusters hung,

A virgin scene!—A little while I stood,
Breathing with such suppression of the heart
As joy delights in; and, with wise restraint
Voluptuous, fearless of a rival, eyed
The banquet—or beneath the trees I sate
Among the flowers, and with the flowers I played;
A temper known to those, who, after long
And weary expectations, have been blest
With sudden happiness beyond all hope. . . .
And—with my cheek on one of those green stones
That, fleeced with moss, under the shady trees,
Lay round me, scattered like a flock of sheep—
I heard the murmur and the murmuring sound,
In that sweet mood when pleasure loves to pay
Tribute to ease; and, of its joy secure,
The heart luxuriates with indifferent things,
Wasting its kindliness on stocks and stones,
And on the vacant air.

The general movement of meaning of this passage is irrepressibly clear, and it requires only the lightest of interpretative touches to bring the details into coherent focus. He must, to begin with, "force" his way over "pathless rocks" and "tangled thickets." The scene is hidden, undiscovered, and he must overcome actual difficulties to find the object of his quest by tearing his way to it. Here he is behaving as a traditional adventurer or hero in pursuit of a dangerous and sequestered goal. But once we get to the scene itself, the general role of classical hero and conqueror, of Darius or Alexander, becomes sharper and more distinctively or narrowly featured—he is now playing at being the classical depredator as well, a Tarquin or Tereus, or in a more modern context, a Lovelace.

For the scene is without qualification erotic or sexual, and the experience being transcribed represents, among other things, the admixture or adjacency of the erotic and the aggressive impulses that we must all learn about and learn to live with. Moreover, he depicts himself as a libertine and voluptuary; he takes pleasure in his ability to restrain himself, to hold back, luxuriating, as it were, in the forepleasure of both intensification of desire and delay of gratification. He is no innocent child of nature in this representation. He recalls himself as experiencing sensual power as over against nature, as perceiving a sharpened sense of selfhood, and as becoming aware in himself of that great force that was in times gone by thought of as and called "lust." And we would not be mistaken if we were to see displaced and recombined components of oedipal and preoedipal phases of development in this little scene, for there can be no doubt by now that the young Wordsworth experienced in Nature at various times projected and transmuted images of his parents, both of whom—particularly his mother—he lost at a comparatively young age. (His mother died when he was eight; she is not the "frugal Dame" of the present poem; his father died when he was thirteen.)

But these considerations, pertinent as they are to any extended reading of the poem, are not immediately salient to the dynamics that we are examining here. For following the period of discovery, self-restraint, voluptuous fantasy, and luxurious self-enjoyment, the young boy goes on to consummate and terminate the project that he has constructed for himself.

> Then up I rose,
> And dragged to earth both branch and bough, with crash
> And merciless ravage; and the shady nook
> Of hazels, and the green and mossy bower,
> Deformed and sullied, patiently gave up
> Their quiet being; and unless I now
> Confound my present feelings with the past;
> Ere from the mutilated bower I turned
> Exulting, rich beyond the wealth of kings,
> I felt a sense of pain when I beheld
> The silent trees, and saw the intruding sky.—
> Then, dearest Maiden, move along these shades
> In gentleness of heart; with gentle hand
> Touch—for there is a spirit in the woods.

He performs an act of rape upon the trees; he has had access to a traditional and conventional influxion of masculine aggressive-erotic will and power. He imperatively possesses the virgin hazels, even as he deforms and sullies and mutilates them—as we do in so many of our fundamental transactions with the world of others, both natural and human. And what he feels, predominantly, he recalls, is exultation, "rich beyond the wealth of kings." Yet at the same time he feels a "sense of pain." In other words, he apprehends "a sense of pain" along with his newly acquired perception of power. If we ask what this ambivalence consists of, we can find it located in his beholding "the silent trees," and suddenly seeing "the intruding sky." What he is apprehending in a new way, and therefore in some form for the first time, is his distinct separateness from nature—that he is different from it, individuated and apart. And his mixed perception, too, is part of the experiences of growing up. In its way, then, "Nutting" is also a companion piece to "Anecdote for Fathers." In that earlier poem the boy changes and develops by being coerced and violated by his unknowing foster father. In "Nutting," the boy enters or catches glimpses of a new phase of development by being himself the active agent of aggression and violation.

If we want to put the matter in more specifically psychoanalytic terms we can say that in this poem the boy has entered a stage of development in which he has become intensely preoccupied with special conceptions of himself (the role playing, the conscious masculine identification, the awareness of depredation and guilt, and so on). As part of this stage he has ceased to be aware of Nature as anything other than an entity not himself which is there to serve the purposes of his will and pleasure. When his unremitting pleasure-seeking leads him to transgress and violate Nature (which he had originally conceived or experienced as part of himself, as a primitive proto-object of identification, or self-object), then he also feels a "sense of pain" and comes to recognize Nature as sentient, as an actual or full object, a violation of which is analogous to a violation of something as alive as himself.

Perhaps I can move toward a conclusion by citing Erik Erikson on the age of dramatic play in childhood. Erikson observes that at this age the child paradigmatically creates a micro-reality for himself, in which he can escape both adult demands and ritualizations of behavior, and prepare his own future reality, reliving, correcting, and re-creating past experience, and anticipating future roles and events with that combination of spontaneity and repetitiveness that characterizes all ritualizations.[2] The themes of this phase of play, he goes on to say, are often dominated by the ideas of *usurpation* and *impersonation* of adult roles. And the principal inner distress or estrangement that finds expression, aggravation, or resolution in play is the sense of guilt. This inescapable sense, he observes, does not even wait for the fantasied deed to be committed; or if committed, to be known to others (as in this poem), or if known to others, to be punished by them. This same theme, he concludes with a characteristic flourish, dominates the great tragedies of our civilizations, for the theater is adult man's "play." And this is particularly true for the dominant form of tragedy in our culture's theater: the conflict between hubris or presumption and guilt—as in *Oedipus Rex,* say—between the usurpation of father-likeness and punishment, between freedom and sin or transgression. Hence the adult stage of this phase of growth is both in part an analogy to and a continuation of the "play" of the child.

Yet that does not end one's dealings with "Nutting," of course. For the poem which begins in play ends in something other. It ends in an awareness of guilt, separateness, and mild admonition, even as it is aware in is own way of such matters as Erikson is adverting to. Like other art and literature, then, it begins in play, in formal gestures, in ritual, and ends with something else, with a new awareness of some condition of existence, with a new sense of the range and capacities of humanity's circumstances.

If we ask how it was that Wordsworth came to apprehend such things at the time he did, we are faced with something of a mystery. Perhaps the best I can do is to suggest that, according to his own testimony, he retained until surprisingly late in childhood some perception of the omnipotence of his own thought, and that even as a seasoned schoolboy he recalled having to clutch at external objects—walls and trees—to assure himself that they were materially real and not part of the internal representations of his own mind. In this way, it may be, he remained in exceptionally close touch with those infantile and childhood modes of mental experience which form the nucleus of his creative powers and to which this exposition has devoted so cursory an examination.

Notes

The Edith Weigert Lecture, sponsored by the Forum on Psychiatry and the Humanities, Washington School of Psychiatry, October 21, 1983.

1. In *Three Essays on the Theory of Sexuality*, Freud pertinently writes, "There are thus good reasons why a child sucking at its mother's breast has become the prototype of every relation of love. The finding of an object is in fact a refinding of it" (*S.E.* 7:222).

2. In a note, Wordsworth remarks that although in the poem he speaks of one day "from many singled out," in fact, "these verses arose out of the remembrance of feelings I had often had when a boy," implying that the result was multiphasic and put together out of several occasions of such experiences.

References

Freud, Sigmund. *The Standard Edition of the Complete Psychological Works*. Edited and translated by James Strachey. London: Hogarth, 1953–74.
   The Interpretation of Dreams (1900), vol. 4.
   Three Essays on the Theory of Sexuality (1905), vol. 7.
Plumb, J. H. "The New World of Children in Eighteenth-Century England." *Past and Present* 67 (1975): 64–93.

2   Lullabies and Child Care:
     A Historical Perspective

Nicholas Tucker

One of the problems babies and infants have always set any community is their tendency to wake up crying during the day or night. If the reason for this is hunger, a quick feed may be all that is required, but other causes of crying, such as pain, fear, or boredom, will not necessarily be appeased in this way. In such cases, it is often impossible to let a baby cry itself to sleep again, since apart from all humane considerations, an infant's bawling at full blast is always a painfully nerve-racking sound for anyone within reasonable earshot (thus making it the effective alarm call it is from the moment of birth onward). Yet if this urgent summons still causes parents problems today in the more spacious accommodations common in the Western world, how much worse it must have been for families living in very cramped conditions in the past, especially those whose economic welfare was dependent on the physical labors of hard-worked fathers and sons, themselves needing all the sleep they could possibly get.

Not surprisingly, therefore, mothers and nurses have always used different methods of getting a baby back to sleep as quickly as possible, particularly when inadequate food supplies make it impractical for a baby to gorge itself back to slumber. One was to dope a baby with poppy syrup or some other sleep-inducing narcotic. The British Medical Association estimated in 1867, for example, that the largely agricultural counties of Lincolnshire and Norfolk consumed between them more than half the total amount of opium imported into Britain around then for precisely this purpose (Horn, 1974, p. 169). Another unpleasant remedy was rocking the cradle so violently that the baby was eventually knocked unconscious: the so-called forceful shaking quoted by Edward Shorter in his provocative study, *The Making of the Modern Family* (1976, p. 172).

17

Both these methods, however, are extreme, and most nursing mothers or their substitutes have usually turned to less dangerous means of bringing about sleep in a way that seems more natural both to adult and child. As it happens, the gentle rocking of a baby at around 60 cycles per minute soon leads to a sharp decline in heart rate, more regular breathing, and a return to sleep (Bowlby, 1973, p. 218). At the same time, a moderate level of auditory stimulation is also soothing to the infant, inducing low activity and drowsiness in its own right (as Pavlov discovered in the case of his dogs, where every monotonous and continuous stimulation led to similar sleepiness). And so, at least where human beings are concerned, the stage is set for the worldwide singing of the lullaby, that powerful combination of sound and movement always so successful in getting babies off to sleep, however often they have heard it before.

Given that restless babies react best to a steady, constant rhythm, it comes as no surprise to discover that most lullaby tunes prefer strict metronomic regularity. Chopin's famous *Berceuse,* for example, shares this unrelenting rhythm in its bass notes, eschewing anything unpredictable and therefore potentially nonsoporific in effect. Other, unmusical sounds that share this steady, monotonous rhythm, such as a metronome itself, or a recording of paired heartbeats or of the steady pulsating of blood rushing through the mother's aorta as it passes by the uterus, together with the smoother, more even sound of the pulsating umbilical cord, can also be effective in putting a baby to sleep. A potent lullaby, therefore, could simply consist of a similarly monotonous mixture of sound and rhythm, such as the seesaw repetition of two notes found among certain North and South American Indians, whose women wordlessly croon their babies to sleep in this way. But as the Spanish poet Lorca once wrote, few mothers want to be mere snake charmers where their babies are concerned (Garcia Lorca, 1930, p. 12). So just as a mother will talk to a new baby long before speech is established, taking its smiles or gurgles for replies, so too will she sing lullabies stretching out into several different verses, where relatively complex verbal messages alternate with the constant iteration of various sleep words such as "lulla," "lalla," and many others.

Since the baby will not understand the actual words sung, and given that no other audience is intended for these occasions, a mother on her own can be fairly uninhibited in what she croons to her infant in the combination of hushed voice and personal privacy most appropriate to singing a baby to sleep. In this sense, immemorial lullabies, handed down via the oral tradition, do not share the qualities of more self-conscious artistic expression where references to or depictions of childhood are concerned. The pictures and sculptures of the Madonna and Child produced in Florence during the early Renaissance, for example, portray a markedly idealized version of the mother-child relationship at a time when real children were "probably lying swaddled and immobile, often miserable and underfed, at the mercy of a wet-nurse, miles away from . . . mother" (Ross, 1974, p. 199). Clearly, art patrons at the time preferred the romantic view of maternal affection depicted by their favorite artists to grim reality itself, just as nineteenth-century British audiences were later to develop a taste for pictures featuring impossibly glamorized child beggars. Here, as elsewhere, art can always offer compensation for what is really happening in society, rather than providing a mirror image for it.

Attitudes toward the baby found in traditional lullabies, however, always appear more convincing—at least, until such lullabies began to be especially composed or generally prettified by collectors during the eighteenth century and after. Before then, as a working tool handed down from mother to mother over the years, the lullaby hailed from distant, anonymous sources, which far from making any public display of "approved" attitudes toward the young, offered mothers and nurses a selection of very personal, sometimes earthy responses to their particular situation. At times the words involved can be tender; at times they can be harsh; but in all events they generally embody a direct, immediate reaction to the task in hand whose honesty seems quite unmistakable.

I would claim, therefore, that those texts of traditional lullabies that have survived offer a rare insight into the minds and hearts of otherwise anonymous mothers from the past. This is something worth attending to, since most of these mothers would never have kept diaries, written letters, or indeed left any other trace of their actual baby-care practices and attitudes for future generations to ponder. This lack of written evidence has sometimes led historians to make vast generalizations about early forms of mothering based on only a very few sources and taking no account of lullaby evidence at all. This is surely a pity, even though it must be admitted that like most examples of folk culture, many lullabies—however old—only got into print comparatively recently, and there is always a reluctance among historians to use sources whose longevity cannot be proved beyond any possible doubt. But today there are a number of social historians quite content to work backward into history from more recently assembled evidence, following the example set by the great French scholar Marc Bloch. Bloch himself first used this so-called regressive method to deduce the history of the French peasantry from the patterns of the fields they tilled. While evidence for this study dating from the eighteenth century was ample, at a time when field maps had become common, records before this time were sparse. Yet Bloch was able to work back to medieval times by an analysis of the eighteenth-century sources and the clear evidence these bore of earlier patterns of owner-ship (1964, p. ix).

More recently, the British historian Peter Burke has demonstrated how the systematic collection of ancient ballads and sources during the eighteenth century can again be used as a basis from which to consider and assess more fragmentary evidence about those of earlier times (1978). In my turn, I too would argue that traditional lullabies collected during the last two centuries, often from relatively unchanged peasant cultures, can indeed tell us a great deal not simply about those peasants themselves, but also about what their remote ancestors would once have been singing. The way that the great mass of traditional lullabies always tends to fall into one of three very similar categories wherever they are tracked down also argues for a certain persistence of theme and approach over time. Evidence for this repetitive pattern can be found in over one hundred traditional lulla-bies collected by the British folklorist Leslie Daiken. All the lullabies he has assembled can be classified under three distinct headings. He writes:

[A mother's] method with this vocal "piece of equipment" may be divided into three distinct approaches. (1) She may try out a lullaby full of blandishments and endearment. (2) Alternatively, her feelings of generos-ity may run to extravagant promises. The promises range from gifts and rewards to what must be accepted as a form of innocent bribery! (3) If bribery fails to get the desired effect, inner desperation may lead a mother to try a lullaby designed for babies who know what's what—the lullaby of threat! [1959, p. 21]

Taking the last point first, it should hardly surprise anyone that a note of resentment should at times enter into lullabies sung by those who are themselves losing sleep. Daiken quotes a Spanish version, for example, where an angry mother sings to her baby: "Go away! You are not my child, your mother was a gypsy" (p. 11). Others, from the same collection, threaten a naughty baby with various vengeful mon-sters, as in this British example:

Baby, baby, naughty baby,
Hush you squalling thing, I say.
Peace this moment, peace, or maybe
Bonaparte will pass this way.

Baby, baby, he's a giant,
Tall and black as Rouen steeple,
And he breakfasts, dines, rely on't,
Every day on naughty people.
[p. 25]

Other bogeymen in British lullabies include Oliver Cromwell, Judge
Jeffreys, Kaiser Wilhelm, and Adolf Hitler, while French babies have
been threatened by Wellington and Bismarck as well as werewolves.
Spanish lullabies frighten their young with El Coco, a black man who
eats babies, and with the Bull, the She-wolf, and the Moorish Queen.
Whether a baby actually understands such threats is not the point; it
is the vicarious relief to the mother, putting her anger into such
punitive phrases, that is important here.

But since the mother singing all these blood-curdling threats is still
trying to get her baby back to sleep, she cannot afford to let an
obviously angry, obtrusive note creep into either the manner in which
she is singing or the steady rhythm with which she is still rocking her
infant. Her voice must remain soothing and her hand steady; small
wonder that the words she chooses sometimes stand in such stark
contrast to the way in which they have to be delivered. In that sense, it
is not too strong to describe some lullabies as exercises in controlled
hatred.

Allied to the lullaby of threat is the lullaby of complaint, often
intensely moving in its self-portrait of a mother or nurse nearing the
end of her tether. Whether life as depicted in such lullabies was
always as bleak as this, or whether these are the extra gloomy feelings
that most often come to mind with a baby persistently crying at night,
is impossible to say. One such British lullaby, first recorded in 1784,
combines the mother's sorrow with a fear for the baby:

Bye, O my baby,
When I was a lady,
O then my baby didn't cry;
But my baby is weeping
For want of good keeping,
O I fear my poor baby will die.
[Opie, 1951, p. 59]

An Italian lullaby of this type accuses rather than pities the baby:

Hushaby; but if thou hast not sleep, hear me,
Thou has robbed me of my heart and of all feeling.
I really cannot think what is your cause for lament

That you are never done lamenting.
[Daiken, p. 15]

A third, Spanish example, sings hopelessly about errant husbands as well as the general sadness of life itself:

Hush, poor child, hush thee to sleep,
Thy father is at the tavern;
Oh the sin and the shame of it all!
Home at midnight he will stagger,
Drunk with strong wine of Navarre.
[Daiken, p. 15]

In other lullabies, however, mothers indulge in fantasies of wish fulfillment, for themselves, their babies, or both, so passing the time rather more cheerfully, as in this British example, first recorded in 1805:

Rock-a-bye, baby,
Thy cradle is green,
Father's a nobleman,
Mother's a queen;
And Betty's a lady,
And wears a gold ring;
And Johnny's a drummer,
And drums for the king.
[Opie, p. 62]

In another well-known lullaby, first written down in 1784, the mother concentrates on the baby rather than on herself:

Bye, baby bunting,
Daddy's gone a-hunting,
Gone to get a rabbit skin
To wrap the baby bunting in.
[Opie, p. 63]

Other treats promised to babies in lullabies recorded elsewhere in Europe include a cake made of honey, spices and rye flour, a funny Polichinello, some best clothes, flowers, and—back in the British Isles again—a fishie on a little dishie from Scotland.

That some of these bribes could certainly have existed in reality, even in the poorest homes, suggests that some mothers have always wanted to provide their babies with special treats from time to time.

Elsewhere, the bribes mentioned are more obviously a case of the mother offering compensatory fantasies to the baby and to herself, once again playing the game that tiny wordless infants could actually understand the nature of all these promises held out to them, and so become quieter at the prospect of such pleasures. In a few cases, there could also be an element of aggression contained in the more extravagant, unreal promises held out to the baby, equivalent to the traditional verbal tricks that adults have always inflicted on children, whereby hopes are first raised and then dashed again.

Apart from bribes, threats, and possible teases, there are also many examples of simple, unadorned tenderness toward babies within a number of traditional lullabies. The fact that mothers sang such songs to themselves and their babies when they were alone must surely clear them of the charge of merely play-acting at affection here. This point is worth stressing, since a particular school of history has recently developed the theme that mother love for infants, at least in Europe, is an invention of the seventeenth and eighteenth centuries. Before that, according to Lloyd de Mause, "The history of childhood is a nightmare from which we have only recently begun to awaken. The further back in history one goes, the lower the level of child care" (1974, p. 1). For Edward Shorter, the situation was equally bad: "Good mothering is an invention of modernisation. In traditional societies, mothers viewed the development and happiness of infants younger than two with indifference" (p. 170). More recently, support for this argument has also come from certain feminist historians, notably Elizabeth Badinter (1981) and Ann Dally (1982).

But this interpretation of earlier forms of motherhood cannot be sustained for all mothers when the evidence of lullabies is taken into account. The powerful endearments they contain must in themselves be evidence of strong, affectionate maternal feeling. According to Daiken, "You are my rose" is widespread in France, Spain, Italy, Greece; for the babe is always likened to the prettiest flower—carnation, gillyflower, rosebud (1959, p. 22). This is not the language of indifference, nor are the numerous endearing epithets applied to the Infant Savior found in Sicilian cradle songs (Martinengo-Cesaresco, 1886, p. 237). Paying affectionate homage to Jesus may not be the same thing as loving one's own child, especially when it is squalling at night, but the language of affection for any baby, even a holy one, cannot grow out of an emotional vacuum.

It could be argued, however, that Italian peasants have always loved their babies more than many other parents, and that much of the evidence cited by de Mause and Shorter comes from sterner British or French sources. Certainly, various foreign visitors to Britain in the past have sometimes remarked on the coolness shown toward children there, and a foremost scholar of English lullabies has written eloquently about "the feature of the Anglo-Saxon temperament which has undergone least modification by Christian and foreign cultural influences; the taste for melancholy brooding of the type that finds expression in elegy. . . . In the lullabies of the present anthology it is mirrored as clearly and continuously as in any series of poems in the language" (Budd, 1930, p. 1). Does it follow, then, that for British children, at least, the experience of mothering was indeed a harsh and melancholy one?

Once again, study of purely British lullabies fails to bear this hypothesis out. While there are a number of angry lullabies and tough, occasionally brutal nursery rhymes concerning children, there have also always been those portraying much gentler feelings. One lullaby carol, for example, first recorded in the fifteenth century, has as its refrain:

> Lullay, myn lykyng, my dere sone, myn swetying,
> Lullay, myn dere herte, myn owyn dere derlying.
> [Greene, 1962]

It would have been impossible to dream up a language of such poignant affection out of nothing. Since other lullaby carols of this time are known to have taken their refrains from already existing secular lullabies, the same could easily be the case in this particular example. Other nonreligious lullabies collected in the British Isles also contain clear indications of love for the baby. This example, *The Washing Song,* translated from the Manx Gaelic *Arrane Ny Niee* in 1921, was described by its local singer at the time, James Kelly, as one that "the young women always used to sing when washing their babies. He maintains that they learned it first from the fairies, who had been heard singing it as they washed their own babies in the early morning in the Awin Ruy, a small river near his farm."

> Hushabye, my darling,
> Hushabye, my darling,
> Hands now I'll wash them,
> Feet now I'll wash them.
> Handsome you, my young one,
> Fair and smooth your body,
> Clothes made of silk so fine,
> Each day puts beauty on you.
> Darling sweet, with hair a-curling,
> King of stars, blessings on you

O my heart, my joy.
[Kennedy, 1975]

Turning to another corner of Britain, Daiken quotes John Jones, in his *Arte and Science of Preserving Bodie and Soule in health, wisedome and Catholike Religion* (1579), as saying, "The best nurses, but especially the trim and skilfull Welch women, doe use to sing some preaty sonets" (1959, p. 62). The various examples of Welsh lullabies quoted by Daiken himself fully bear out this sentiment, as do examples collected by different scholars. One such, *Suo Gan,* "began to turn up in song collections in 1800" (Cole, 1969). Its rather flowery modern translation goes like this:

Sleeping baby, on my bosom, warm and comfy it will prove;
Round thee mother's arms are folding, in her heart a mother's love
There shall no-one come to harm thee, naught shall ever break thy rest
Sleep my darling babe, in quiet; sleep on mother's gentle breast.

Scotland, too, has its share of loving lullabies, such as "Balaloo," described by its editor as "an old Scottish cradle song." It, too, has a moving first verse:

Now balloo, lammy, now balloo, my dear,
Now balaloo, Lammy, ain mammie is here.
What ails my wee bairnie? What ails it this night?
What ails my wee lammy? Is bairnie no right?
[Kidson, 1897]

In a country like Scotland, whose rural inhabitants still possess family traditions that go very far back and who sometimes occupy the same land as their ancestors in the seventeenth century, the "regressive" method of working through more recently recorded lullabies back to their ancient originals seems particularly appropriate.

All this is not to suggest that lullabies prove that once all mothers always loved their babies most of the time. There have always been individual variations in the ways different mothers react to babies at any age, and other traditional lullabies suggest the coexistence of a far bleaker form of mother-baby relationship. This is not surprising, since the poverty and overcrowding common in the past would have put a strain upon everyone, often resulting in less affection to spare for numerous, unplanned babies at a time when everyone's life, child or adult, was surely much tougher than would be the case today. Nor can the appalling incidence of cruelty to small children in the past be overlooked. There were fit young mothers who still banished their babies to the occasionally murderous negligence of wet nurses in the country. Elsewhere, standards of care in baby farms and foundling hospitals could be practically nonexistent, with only intermittent protest from outside, even from those living near such places who must have known at least something about what was going on.

There equally seems no doubt, however, that despite hardship and many other conflicting demands, some mothers seem always to have chosen to sing lullabies which include very affectionate passages at a time when the baby itself could make little of the words and no one else was around to judge whether this was an especially suitable thing to do. Nurses, too, chose from the same selection, for it was often their job to sing to the crying baby while the mother was elsewhere and therefore unable to feed it. There are lullabies plainly designed to be sung by mother substitutes that contain the same mixture of endearment, anger, despair, and cajoling, suggesting that loving a baby, among other emotions, was not simply something expected of a mother alone. Elsewhere, there are some affectionate lullabies aimed specifically at baby girls, proving that it was not only baby boys who were loved at a time when values tended to be overwhelmingly patriarchal.

It is revealing to note the way in which modern historians have neglected lullabies as a relevant source. But like ancient adult-baby games, such as knee riding, pat-a-cake, face tapping, or knee tickling, lullabies are part of that lore handed down from mother to baby usually in the privacy of the home rather than on public display. Adult male commentators, anxious at any period to pronounce on what mothers should or should not be doing with their children, may often have missed these little songs and games altogether, just as predominantly male historians today also ignore their significance. For myself, the many lullabies that illustrate more positive feelings clearly suggest that there have always been some gentler moments between mothers and babies, in addition to the resentment and exhausted hopes naturally caused when a mother or nurse is forced to lose too much sleep. Looking at traditional lullabies as a whole reveals a spread of emotion not very different from the conflicting feelings babies also give rise to in our own times. On this evidence, there is no need to believe, with some historians, that any baby born more than three hundred years ago or so would necessarily have missed out on expressions of mother love altogether, or that their twentieth-century counterparts always do so much better in this department at the hands of modern parents.

References

Badinter, Elizabeth. *The Myth of Motherhood: An Historical View of the Maternal Instinct*. London: Souvenir Press, 1981.

Bloch, Marc. *Les caractères originaux de l'histoire rurale française*. Paris: Colin, 1964.

Bowlby, John. *Attachment,* vol. 1. London: Hogarth, 1973.

Budd, Frederick E., ed. *A Book of Lullabies 1300–1900*. London: Eric Partridge, Scholastic Press, 1930.

Burke, Peter. *Popular Culture in Early Modern Europe*. London: Temple Smith, 1978.

Cole, William, *Folksongs of England, Ireland, Scotland and Wales*. London: Hansen, 1969.

Daiken, Leslie. *The Lullaby Book*. London: Edmund Ward, 1959.

Dally, Ann. *Inventing Motherhood: The Consequences of an Ideal*. London: Burnett Books, 1982.

de Mause, Lloyd, ed. *The History of Childhood*. New York: Psychohistory Press, 1974.

Garcia Lorca, Federico. *Deep Song and Other Prose*. Edited and translated by C. Maurer. London: Marion Boyars, 1980.

Greene, Richard, ed. *A Selection of English Carols*. Oxford: Clarendon Press, 1962.

Horn, Pamela. *The Victorian Country Child*. London: Kineton, 1974.

Kennedy, Peter, ed. *Folksongs of Britain and Ireland*. London: Cassell, 1975.

Kidson, Frank, ed. *Children's Songs of Long Ago*. London: Augener, 1897.

Martinengo-Cesaresco, Evelyn. *Essays in the Study of Folk-lore*. London: J. M. Dent, 1896.

Opie, Iona, and Opie, Peter. *The Oxford Dictionary of Nursery Rhymes*. Oxford: Oxford University Press, 1951.

Ross, James Bruce. "The Middle-class Child in Urban Italy, Fourteenth to Early Sixteenth Century," in de Mause (1974).

Shorter, Edward. *The Making of the Modern Family*. London: Collins, 1976.

3　From Nags to Witches: Stepmothers in the Grimms' Fairy Tales

Maria Tatar

Fairy tales, as the first sentence of the celebrated collection assembled by the Brothers Grimm tells us, take place "in the olden days, when wishing was still of use" (Steig, 1912, p. 1). Oddly enough, however, in reviewing the 210 tales that compose the *Kinder- und Hausmärchen* for examples of explicitly stated wishes, it becomes evident that fairy-tale figures are far more likely to utter curses on their enemies than to express wishes for themselves. In the olden days, it would appear, wishing may still have been of use, but cursing figured as the preferred mode of verbal utterance.

The curses voiced in fairy tales generally take the form of magical spells—spells that transform princes into frogs or bears, sons into ravens or swans, and brothers into stags or lambs. One single verbal pronouncement or isolated act suffices to effect the metamorphosis of a boy into a beast. Nearly all the stock characters of fairy tales (with the exception of the young male victims) are blessed or cursed with this gift of casting spells. When a father, for example, denounces his sons in a moment of irritation for their frivolous ways and utters the fateful wish that they turn into ravens, he finds himself endowed with magical powers. No sooner has the wish escaped his lips than he hears the beating of wings and silently watches seven ravens fly off into the distance. Variants of the tale of the seven ravens suggest that such heedless imprecations, whether uttered by fathers or by mothers, are instantly translated into reality. In "Twelve Brothers," it is the sister of the twelve boys who bears the blame for their transformation into ravens, though some versions of that tale implicate the children's stepmother in the guilty act. In yet another tale of enchanted male siblings ("Six Swans"), a woman turns her stepsons into winged creatures when she flings six magical shirts over them.

28

While the spells cast in these three tales are all equally effective, only one of the three transformations arises from a willful act of premeditated evil. It is the stepmother alone who deliberately takes advantage of magical powers to harm her six stepchildren. Nearly the entire cast of characters in fairy tales may possess magical powers, yet it will be obvious to the habitual reader of these tales that stepmothers are nonetheless the principal agents of enchantment. Or perhaps it would be more accurate to state that mothers in their various incarnations as stepmother, witch, and mother-in-law stand as the chief source of evil in these tales even as they stand as the chief source of good when they make an appearance as fairy godmother, wise woman, or Holy Virgin. Actual biological mothers, however, seldom command a central role in the fairy tales collected by the Brothers Grimm, in part because Wilhelm Grimm could rarely resist the temptation to act as censor by turning the monstrously unnatural mothers of these tales into stepmothers.[1] But stepmothers abound at the homes of fairy-tale heroes; witches masquerading as magnanimous mothers are nearly ubiquitous in the woods; and evil mothers-in-law inevitably make their presence felt in the castles that serve as a second home for fairy-tale heroines.

Stepmother, witch, and mother-in-law: these are the various labels used to designate a character who takes on a single well-defined function in fairy tales and whose role is limited to the sphere of action known as villainy. That these three figures share not only a common function but also a single identity becomes clear on closer scrutiny of various tales. In "Brother and Sister," for example, the stepmother is in reality a witch who has cunningly insinuated herself into the household. At home she subjects her stepchildren to daily abuse; in the forest she continues to tyrannize them by hexing their every source of drinking water. In "Hansel and Gretel," it is probably not merely coincidental that the two siblings return home to find that their cruel stepmother has vanished once they have conquered the evil witch in the woods.[2] Stepmothers are not always so neatly eradicated once the stepchildren find their way out from the woods. The heroine who emerges from the forest to live happily ever after with the king who found her there frequently finds her domestic bliss disturbed by a sinister mother-in-law, by her own spiteful stepmother, or—as in "Twelve Brothers"—by a figure who is described first as the heroine's mother-in-law, then as her stepmother.[3] It quickly becomes clear that stepmother, witch, and mother-in-law are only different names for a single villain whose aim it is to banish the heroine from hearth and home and to subvert her elevation from humble origins to a noble status. What at first blush appears to be a conspiracy of hags and witches is in the final analysis the work of a single female villain.

The female villain of fairy tales operates in three separate and distinct arenas of action that emerge in chronological sequence. The main contours of the opening situation in those tales that feature stepmothers are reasonably predictable. The child or children whose biological mother has died become the victims of a brutal, scheming stepmother. As one fairy-tale brother confides to his sister: "Ever since mother died, we haven't had an hour of peace; our stepmother beats us every day, and whenever we go up to her, she kicks us away" (Steig, 1912, p. 37). Small wonder that these abused adolescents resolve to escape the oppressive atmosphere at home even at the cost of facing the perils of "the vast world." Those who fail to move into voluntary exile are, like Hansel and Gretel, banished from home owing to a stepmother's skillful bullying of her husband. But even those who patiently endure villainy at home find themselves expelled from the family circle, living like servants at the hearth rather than like children at home. Whether at home or in the woods, the once unrivaled princes and princesses of the household find themselves dethroned, living a lowly existence in exile. Whether literally of royal parentage or simply regal by virtue of their status as children, the adolescent protagonists of fairy tales find that their legitimate rights have been abrogated and their positions have been usurped by those perennial pretenders to the throne known in fairy tales as stepsisters.[4]

If home represents the first station in the hero's sufferings, the enchanted world of the forest stands as the locus of his second series of struggles. But in the woods the hero is no longer pitted against an all-powerful human adversary; instead he finds himself locked in combat with a superhuman opponent armed with supernatural powers. The villainous stepmother at home reemerges in the woods as a monster equipped with powers far more formidable than those she exercised at home. If at home she proved adept at deposing her stepchildren and banishing them from the household by constantly badgering and hectoring either children or spouse, in the woods she appears to be above all a master in the art of transforming humans into animals. Yet her power to turn children into beasts is generally exerted on stepsons; the task of disenchantment itself falls to stepdaughters. Brother rather than sister is turned into a deer when he drinks from waters enchanted by his stepmother; Hansel, and not Gretel, is encaged and fattened up for a feast of flesh; the six swans in the tale of that title are all male; and of the thirteen royal children in "Twelve Brothers," only the boys find themselves taking wing. In this context, it is worth noting that there are few female counterparts to the many enchanted males in the cycle of tales known as animal-groom stories. To be sure, female heroines are not immune to the spells cast by evil witches and fairies, but, like Snow White and Sleeping Beauty, they remain eternally human and beautiful even in their dormant, enchanted states. That brothers and prospective bridegrooms are turned into animals by older women may be read as a telling commentary on women's attitudes toward male sexuality, just as the choice of a catatonic Snow White and Sleeping Beauty as the fairest and most desirable of them all may offer a sobering statement on men's visions of the ideal bride.[5]

While the curses uttered by stepmothers take effect almost instantaneously, the process of disenchantment is both long and arduous. In tales of metamorphosed males, the sisters or prospective brides of the degraded heroes are burdened with the task of disenchantment. Yet as one mentor after another warns these heroines, the conditions of that task are so difficult as to be virtually impossible to fulfill. Only Gretel, who keeps her wits about her, succeeds in liberating her brother within a reasonable period of time. The sister of the six swans requires a more typical time span; she spends year after year perched on a tree branch silently sewing shirts and releases her brothers from the stepmother's curse only after six years have passed. Given the duration of the brothers' bewitchment, it is not altogether surprising to find that the heroine of the fairy tale matures, marries, and establishes a family of her own by the time the prescribed length of her trial has elapsed.

Even while the brothers of fairy-tale heroines patiently wait in the woods for liberation from their enchanted state, the heroines themselves have moved on to a third arena of action. Rescued or, more often than not, kidnapped by the hunting party of a king, they are spirited off to a castle and in due course married to the sovereign of the land. Yet many of these heroines, who are bound by vows of silence or solemnity, cannot yet live happily ever after—at least not so long as their brothers remain in an enchanted state. Furthermore, even at the castle that has become their second home, they become once again the victims of plotting females, be they treacherous mothers-in-law or ever-vigilant stepmothers who have heard of their stepdaughters' accession to a throne. Since the young queens have themselves frequently become mothers, the murderous schemes of their stepmothers take on an added dimension of peril. For the children of the new royal couple seem destined to share the lot of their mothers, to relive the fairy tale whose plot will come to an end with the death of their biological mother. Once a stepmother succeeds in murdering her stepdaughter (as she does in "Brother and Sister") or in conspiring to have her put to death (as she does in "Twelve Brothers" and "Six Swans"), she paves the way for the marriage of her own biological daughter to the newly widowed king and thereby precisely recreates the kind of family situation that prevailed at the tale's beginning.[6] That new royal family, like the nuclear family described in the opening paragraphs of fairy tales, would consist of a father, a stepmother, and one or more children from the father's first marriage. It can only be a matter of time until the sole missing elements, the children of the second union, appear on the scene to assist in reenacting the drama played out in the first part of the fairy tale.

Before anyone can live happily ever after, this vicious cycle of events must be arrested. To avoid the danger of endless repetitions of one plot, the stepmother must perish along with her mischievous offspring. Not until she has been conquered and done away with is it possible to break the magic spell that bedevils the stepchildren of fairy tales and threatens to doom generation after generation of their progeny. Once a fairy-tale heroine succeeds in reversing the effects of her stepmother's villainy, either by completing the tasks assigned to her or by returning from the dead to broadcast the harm done to her, the process of disenchantment is complete. To emphasize the definitive end to the stepmother's reign of terror, the fairy tale describes her demise in graphic and morbid detail. Drowned, burned to ashes, torn to pieces by wild animals, or placed in a casket filled with boiling oil and poisonous snakes, she dies in both body and spirit and no longer represents a threat to the recently established royal family. And once the biological mother of that family reigns supreme, the king and even his children are destined to live happily ever after.

Stepmothers, it would appear, figure as an abiding source of evil in countless fairy tales, and it is consequently no accident that they rank among the most memorable villains in these tales. Folklorists would no doubt be hard pressed to name a single good stepmother, for in fairy tales the very title "stepmother" pins the badge of iniquity on a figure.[7] One could, in fact, safely argue that the phrase "wicked stepmother" ("böse Stiefmutter"), which has a nearly formulaic ring to it, is itself pleonastic.

Scholars have traced the persistent affiliation between stepmothers and evil to Icelandic folktales, in which tales of cruel stepmothers with magical powers constitute a cardinal genre.[8] The prologues to these folktales tell of a recently widowed king who dispatches messengers to a nearby island to fetch a new queen. Although the envoys lose their way to the island owing to a magically produced fog, they succeed in landing on a foreign isle where they meet a woman of enchanting beauty who consents to become the king's bride. Once that marriage is consummated, the new queen—in reality a wicked witch—begins to make life difficult for her stepchildren. Her curses customarily land, however, not on a stepdaughter, but on her stepson, who is either transformed into an animal or condemned to roam the lands until he finds the one woman whose love and devotion will release him from his enchanted state or end his eternal wanderings. As folklorists have pointed out, the king's union with a woman from foreign lands stands as a violation of endogamy rules and constitutes a transgression of nuptial norms that carries with it grave consequences (Meletinsky, 1974, p. 63). Once a man marries outside his specific tribe or social unit, he brings down upon his family a curse that emanates from the foreign origins of his bride and takes on concrete form in that bride's ill treatment of the children from his first marriage.

In the Grimms' collection of fairy tales, both stepsons and stepdaughters figure as targets of maternal maledictions. But in those tales recounting the search of an enchanted prince for a bride capable of breaking a witch's magic spell, stepmothers and even mothers are often absent from the repertoire of the tale's characters. Yet the prince's transformation into a beast is nonetheless nearly always attributed to an evil woman. Once the Frog King, for example, is restored to his regal human condition, he hastens to tell his bride that an evil witch had cast a spell upon him and that no one but she—the princess standing before him—could have released him from his amphibian state. Although the source of the prince's bewitchment does not constitute a part of the tale's plot and is mentioned more in passing than as a significant episode from the prince's past, there is clearly a story behind it and a history to it. Witches, after all, rarely act capriciously in their choice of victims. Given the thinly veiled identity of most witches in the Grimms' collection of tales and given the folkloric origins of witches in earlier Icelandic tales, it requires no great leap of the imagination to place the blame for the prince's enchanted state squarely on the shoulders of a stepmother.

In the vast majority of German tales in which stepmothers figure as prominent villains, it is the stepdaughter who takes on the role of innocent martyr and patient sufferer. If the stepmother of these tales is not literally a witch, she possesses qualities that place her firmly in the class of ogres and fiends. Like her Icelandic counterpart, she too is an alien intruder who disturbs the harmony among blood relatives. She may not always have the power to perform an actual metamorphosis, but she can turn even the most aristocratic and beguiling girl into the humblest of scullery maids. By contrast to the sorceresses who work behind the scenes, she remains a visible, palpable presence in fairy tales that chart the shifting fortunes of heroines who have lost their biological mothers and await rescue by dashing young princes or kings.

In tales that end with the wedding of a royal couple, stepmothers are repeatedly implicated in the evil that befalls their stepchildren, just as they eternally attempt to obstruct their elevation to a higher social rank. These heartless creatures stand in sharp contrast to their relatively artless spouses, whose only serious defect appears to be a lack of discrimination in choosing a marriage partner. The fathers of fairy-tale heroines may appear to be passive to a fault, yet they never once take the lead in abandoning their children or in treating them like servants. It is the stepmother of Hansel and Gretel who hatches the plot to desert the children in the forest; only after being subjected to a good measure of browbeating does their father acquiesce in her plans. Cinderella's father never conspires to debase his daughter, for his wife and stepdaughters are experts in the art of humiliation. And the father of Snow White (mentioned by the Grimms only in the context of his remarriage and even then solely to motivate the presence of a stepmother) never once interferes with the elaborate witchcraft to which his wife resorts in order to remain "the fairest of them all." Although the fathers of these fairy-tale figures are supremely passive or positively negligent when it comes to their children's welfare, they remain benevolent personages largely because their benign neglect contrasts so favorably to the monstrous deeds of their wives.

In the Grimms' collection of tales there is one conspicuous example of a father whose perversity rivals the malice harbored by his female counterparts in fairy tales. Stepmothers may sin by withholding love and affection from their stepchildren, but this father errs in the excessive love and devotion he feels for his biological daughter. The father of the young Allerleirauh, in the tale that bears her name, promises his wife on her deathbed that he will remarry only if he finds a woman whose beauty equals that of his quickly fading wife. When the king's envoys return from a worldwide search for a second wife to announce that they have failed in their mission, the king's eye lights on his own daughter, and he feels a passionate love ("heftige Liebe") for her. The king's councillors may be stunned by the sovereign's proposal to marry his own daughter, but they are not nearly so shocked and dismayed as Allerleirauh herself who, after a variety of delaying tactics, ultimately flees the castle into the woods to escape her father's incestuous advances.

If the tales in which children are banished from hearth and home owing to a stepmother's insufficient love are linked to the violation of exogamy rules, those tales in which a child flees home owing to a father's excessive love are clearly linked to the violation of exogamy rules. On the surface of things it would appear that plots concerned with alien stepmothers are utterly incompatible with plots featuring incestuous fathers, particularly since the two plots have their origins in the violation of diametrically opposed marital norms. Yet on reflection, it becomes clear that the two tale types can, with only minor modifications, coexist as one drama. Antti Aarne's authoritative register of tale types in fact assigns a single number to both plots (1910 and 1928, pp. 81–82).

In German tales depicting social persecution of a daughter by her stepmother, the central focus comes to rest on the unbearable family situation produced by a father's remarriage. But while the father's transgression of marital norms often recedes into the background or is entirely suppressed as a motif even as the father himself is virtually eliminated as a character, the foul deeds of his wife come to occupy center stage. In tales depicting erotic persecution of a daughter by her father, on the other hand, mothers and stepmothers tend to disappear from the central arena of action. Yet the father's forbidden incestuous desire for his daughter in the second tale type furnishes a powerful motive for the stepmother's jealous rages and unnatural deeds in the first tale type. The two plots thereby conveniently dovetail to produce an intrigue that corresponds almost perfectly to the oedipal fantasies of female children. In practice, however, it becomes evident that intimations of a father's special fondness for his daughter are discreetly kept to a minimum while the evil deeds of a stepmother are inevitably writ large.

As Bruno Bettelheim has pointed out, fairy tales enacting female oedipal conflicts tend to split the mother into two figures: a preoedipal good mother who stands by her child and an oedipal evil stepmother who stands in the way of the female child's attempts to secure the love of her father (the prince or king of fairy tales) (1977). To be sure, the vast majority of tales with heroines persecuted by stepmothers also either portray benevolent maternal figures in the form of wise women or, failing that, enact a deceased mother's undying love for her child by bringing Mother Nature to the heroine's rescue. Cinderella, the Goose Girl, Allerleirauh, and a host of other oppressed female protagonists benefit either from nature's munificence or from the natural sanctuaries found in the hollows of trees and in the forest itself.[9] Yet while the good mother generally appears incognito as a dove, a cow, or a tree, the evil stepmother, even when she is a royal personage, is almost invariably designated by her maternal title and stands as a flesh-and-blood embodiment of maternity in the tale. It is this figure of manifest evil who is thus most openly associated with women in their roles as mothers.

If the Grimms' fairy tales tend to permit all manner of explicit social persecution by jealous stepmothers (whose real identity is only thinly concealed by the prefix "step-"), they also tend to avoid direct depiction of erotic persecution by fathers. At home, fathers are either absent or so passive as to be virtually superfluous figures. Only in the tale of Allerleirauh does a father stand as the active source of evil at home, with the consequence that the theme of incest is both broached and pushed to its limits. Even the most restrained commentators on "Allerleirauh" concede that the heroine ends by marrying the very king who sent her into exile. "The Grimms' description [of this event]," as one early critic put it, "is so ambiguous—evidently intentionally ambiguous so as to avoid being offensive—that the true meaning is concealed, though by no means suppressed."[10]

At times it appears as if the tellers of these tales, or at least those who set down the tales in their written versions, were bent on excising all explicit references to the source of rivalry that divides mothers from daughters in childhood fantasies. As folklorists remind us, censorship of material in oral literature is, however, generally exercised by the audience for a tale, which determines the vitality of certain plots by voicing approval of them or simply by selecting them for retelling.[11] In our own culture, we find this process of selection working manifestly in favor of the rags-to-riches tale that contains a wicked older woman. "Cinderella," "Snow White," and "Sleeping Beauty" are the tales from the Grimms' collection that continue to thrive even on non-native soil, while a tale such as "Allerleirauh" is virtually unknown.[12] Of the two components that shape female oedipal plots—the fantasy of an amorously inclined father and the fantasy of rivalry with the mother—only the latter has become a prominent, virtually undisguised theme in popular tales depicting the marriage of female protagonists. While (step)mothers are habitually demonized as nags at home and as witches in the woods, fathers qua fathers tend to fade into the background or to be entirely absent from the tale.

In this context, it is important to bear in mind that the passive or absent father was not always the rule in fairy tales. As Marian Cox's study of 345 variants of "Cinderella" makes clear, there were at least two widespread and pervasive versions of that tale which attributed the heroine's degradation either to an "unnatural father" or to a father who attempts to extract a confession of love from his daughter (1967). Of the 226 tales belonging unambiguously to the three categories labeled by Cox as (1) ill-treated heroine (with mothers, stepmothers, and their progeny as victimizers), (2) unnatural father, and (3) King Lear judgment, 130 belong to the first class and 96 to the next two classes. Thus in the number of extant tales examined by Cox in 1892, the versions that cast (step)mothers in the role of villain only slightly outnumber those that ascribe Cinderella's misfortunes to an importunate father. Cinderella is therefore almost as likely to flee the household because of her father's perverse erotic attachment to her as she is to be banished to the hearth and degraded to servitude by an ill-tempered stepmother.

While critics have correctly argued that it is impossible to reconstruct the *Urmärchen*, or authentic original tale (if ever there was one), that gave rise to the countless versions of "Cinderella" existing all over the world, it is important to recognize that one basic tale type has attached to it two themes that are now perceived to be competing entities. The jealous mother and amorous father, as Cox's neat divisions make clear, rarely coexist in one tale. In "Aschenputtel," the Grimms' version of "Cinderella," the father makes only the briefest of cameo appearances to give his daughter a branch which, once planted, turns into a tree that showers Cinderella with royal apparel for the ball. From an accomplice in Cinderella's degradation, he has turned into an unwitting, yet nonetheless benevolent, helper in the tests that await her. In "Allerleirauh," by contrast, the only mother figure in the tale expires in the introductory paragraph.

In tales emphasizing a stepmother's cruelty, the role of the biological father tends to remain peripheral. Indeed, the father does not appear at all in a number of stories that conform to the rags-to-riches pattern found in "Cinderella." "Snow White" stands as an especially prominent example of such a tale, although even this most chaste and guileless of fairy-tale heroines is subjected to paternal advances in some versions of her story, even as her father's manifest delight in her beauty stands as the source of marital discord in other versions.[13] In the Grimms' version of the tale, which refers to the father only once and even then merely to proclaim his marriage, astute critics have nonetheless succeeded in identifying vestiges of the father's original function: "His surely is the voice of the looking glass, the patriarchal voice of judgment that rules the Queen's—and every woman's—self-evaluation."[14] Once the disembodied voice in the mirror is recognized as that of the wicked queen's husband, it becomes clear that the struggle between Snow White and her mother is motivated by rivalry for the love and admiration of an absent father and husband.

The voice in the mirror is not the sole means by which the father makes his presence felt in the tale. In his study of fifty-seven variants of the tale of Snow White, Ernst Böklen notes (with evident consternation) that some versions of the tale openly depict the father as a coconspirator in his wife's intrigues (1910, pp. 68–69). It is he who, in an attempt to pacify his disagreeable wife, leads Snow White into the woods and subsequently abandons her there. Böklen's study of such variants gives added weight to the view voiced by Bruno Bettelheim that the hunter who spares Snow White's life yet also abandons her in the woods may represent a disguised father-figure. Torn between his loyalty to a wife and to a daughter, he "tries to placate the mother, by seemingly executing her order, and the girl, by merely not killing her" (Bettelheim, 1977, p. 206). In short, despite the complete suppression in this tale of explicit references to the figure for whose affection mother and daughter vie, the logic of the oedipal subplot dictates the presence of male figures who find themselves divided in their allegiance to a mother and her daughter.

In reviewing the Grimms' tales of oppressed female protagonists, it becomes evident that these stories dramatize female oedipal conflicts in unique fashion. With the exception of "Allerleirauh," they suppress the theme of paternal erotic pursuit even as they indulge freely in elaborate variations on the theme of maternal domestic tyranny. For the one story in the *Kinder- und Hausmärchen* that openly depicts a father's persecution of his daughter, there are twelve that recount a girl's misery at the hands of her stepmother. Enshrining the stepmother as villain brings with it the added advantage of exonerating both biological parents from blame for the miserable conditions at home. One might reasonably argue that cruel stepmothers, absent fathers, and child abandonment counted far more significantly than father-daughter incest among the social realities of the age in which the Grimms recorded German fairy tales.[15] Yet fairy tales have never been treasured as mirrors of reality; only in their opening paragraphs do they offer a world that bears some resemblance to the realities of family life.[16] Once the protagonists of those tales leave home, they pass through the looking glass into a world of inner realities. While those childhood fantasies may possess a remarkable stability by contrast to social realities, they are nonetheless reshaped and modified by the cultural setting in which they are told and retold. In our own age, it is easy to see why fairy tales, which evolved only late in their development into stories for children, favor the theme of maternal malice over the forbidden and forbidding theme of incest.

Notes

1. Therese Poser (1980, p. 89) makes this point. The Grimms' recasting of the tale "Frau Holle" illustrates the tendency to motivate a mother's cruelty to her daughter by turning the daughter into a stepdaughter. The original version of the

tale features a widow with two biological daughters; the second version of 1819 traces the fortunes of a widow with one favored, biological daughter and one ill-treated stepdaughter. Similarly, the first version of "Sneewittchen" casts Snow White's mother in the role of villain, while the second version features a step-mother as Snow White's persecutor.

2. Hedwig von Beit (1960, pp. 133–35) suggests that the two figures (step-mother and witch) are identical. Her argument draws on primitive beliefs that equate the murder of a witch's spiritual essence, whatever form it may take, with the destruction of her physical body.

3. Werner Lincke notes this inconsistency in "Twelve Brothers" (1933, p. 69).

4. On royalty as an emblem of paternity ("le roi du conte n'a pas d'autre royaume que sa propre famille") and the consequent noble status of other family members, see Marthe Robert (1966, pp. 24–34). To make elaborate distinctions between the values of rich and poor in fairy tales, as does Klaus Doderer, seems a fruitless exercise (1969, pp. 136–51).

5. "Since our mothers—or nurses—were our earliest educators, it is likely that they first tabooed sex in some fashion; hence it is a female who turns the future groom into an animal" (Bettelheim, 1977, p. 283). Sandra M. Gilbert and Susan Gubar argue that Snow White in the coffin has become the "eternally beautiful, inanimate *objet d'art* patriarchal aesthetics want a girl to be" (1979, p. 40).

6. Sandra M. Gilbert and Susan Gubar argue, in another context, that the cycle of Snow White's fate is inexorable. Like her stepmother, she too is destined to become "a murderess bent on the self-slaughter implicit in her murderous attempts against the life of her own child" (1979, p. 42). By contrast, Sibylle Birkhäuser-Oeri argues that Snow White's marriage represents "a 'Mysterium Coniunctionis,' i.e., the moment of human fulfillment, the wedding of oppo-sites" (1976, pp. 75–76). On the "false bride" in fairy tales, see Paul Arfert (1897).

7. The exception that proves the rule can be found in Adeline Rittershaus's collection of Icelandic fairy tales. It is worth noting, however, that "the good stepmother," in the tale of that title, does not become a stepmother until the very end of the tale and that she protects her prospective stepdaughter from the posthumous curse of her biological mother (1902, pp. 152–55). I am grateful to my colleague Stephen A. Mitchell for calling this tale to my attention.

8. See especially Werner Lincke (1933, pp. 90–140); Ingeborg Weber-Keller-mann (1974, pp. 32–37); and Eleazer Meletinsky (1974, pp. 61–72). Hannah Kühn draws on folkloric material for her analysis of the roles of stepmothers in family life (1929).

9. Ruth B. Bottigheimer argues that, in fairy tales, "the female's original access to power through her association with nature became perverted and denied, so that more recent versions of fairy tales relegate power held by females to the old, the ugly, and/or wicked" (1980, pp. 1–12). On the association of power with repulsive female figures, see also Marcia R. Lieberman (1972, pp. 383–95). Finally, on the role of the "wise old woman" in the Grimms' fairy tales, see Marthe Robert (1969, pp. 44–56).

10. Erich Wulffen (1910, p. 355). On incest in fairy tales, see also Otto Rank (1926, pp. 337–86).

11. Roman Jakobson and P. Bogatyrev (1966, 4:1–15).

12. Kay Stone states that the tale is usually omitted from anthologies "since the heroine is forced to leave home to avoid her father's threat of incestuous marriage." See "Things Walt Disney Never Told Us" (1975, pp. 42–50).

13. Johannes Bolte and Georg Polívka (1913, 1:461); Ernst Böklen (1910, p. 9).

14. Gilbert and Gubar (1979, p. 38).

15. Louise Bernikow, however, advances the view that the tale of "Allerleirauh" may actually reflect "something of how it was in the world out of which the stories came." That Cinderella's male antagonists are replaced by female persecutors "must have to do with what is congenial to the mind that tells the story" (1980, pp. 18–38).

16. As Vladimir Propp points out, the folktale (by contrast to anecdotes, fables, and novellas) rarely draws on real life for its substance (1968, pp. 234–62).

References

Aarne, Antti. *Verzeichnis der Märchentypen.* Folklore Fellows Communications, no. 3. Helsinki: Academia Scientiarum Fennica, 1910.

———. *The Types of the Folk-tale: A Classification and Bibliography.* Translated and enlarged by Stith Thompson, Folklore Fellows Communications, no. 74. Helsinki: Academia Scientiarum Fennica, 1928.

Arfert, Paul. "Das Motiv von der unterschobenen Braut in der internationalen Erzählungsliteratur." Ph.D. dissertation, University of Rostock, 1897.

Beit, Hedwig von. *Symbolik des Märchens: Versuch einer Deutung.* 2d ed. Bern: Francke, 1960.

Bernikow, Louise. *Among Women.* New York: Harper and Row, Colophon Books, 1980.

Bettelheim, Bruno. *The Uses of Enchantment: The Meaning and Importance of Fairy Tales.* New York: Random House, Vintage Books, 1977.

Birkhäuser-Oeri, Sibylle. *Die Mutter im Märchen. Deutung der Problematik des Mütterlichen und des Mutterkomplexes am Beispiel bekannter Märchen,* ed. Marie-Luise von Franz. Stuttgart: Adolf Bonz, 1976.

Böklen, Ernst. *Sneewittchenstudien: Fünfundsiebzig Varianten im engern Sinn.* Leipzig: J. C. Hinrichs, 1910.

Bolte, Johannes, and Polívka Georg. *Anmerkungen zu den Kinder- und Hausmärchen der Brüder Grimm.* Leipzig: Dieterich, 1913.

Bottigheimer, Ruth B. "The Transformed Queen: A Search for the Origins of Negative Female Archetypes in Grimms' Fairy Tales." *Amsterdamer Beiträge zur neueren Germanistik* 10 (1980): 1–12.

Cox, Marian Roalfe. *Cinderella: Three Hundred and Forty-five Variants of Cinderella, Catskin, and Cap o' Rushes.* 1892; rpt. Nendeln, Liechtenstein: Kraus, 1967.

Doderer, Klaus. "Das bedrückende Leben der Kindergestalten in den Grimmschen Märchen." In *Klassische Kinder- und Jugendbücher. Kritische Betrachtungen.* Wernheim: Julius Betz, 1969.

Gilbert, Sandra M., and Gubar, Susan. *The Madwoman in the Attic: The Woman Writer and the Nineteenth-Century Literary Imagination.* New Haven: Yale University Press, 1979.

Jakobson, Roman, and Bogatyrev, P. "Die Folklore als eine besondere Form des Schaffens." In Roman Jakobson. *Selected Writings.* The Hague: Mouton, 1966.

Kühn, Hannah. "Psychologische Untersuchungen über das Stiefmutterproblem" *Beihefte zur Zeitschrift für angewandte Psychologie,* no. 45. Leipzig: Johann Ambrosius Barth, 1929.

Lieberman, Marcia R. " 'Some Day My Prince Will Come': Female Acculturation Through the Fairy Tale," *College English* 34 (1972): 383–95.

Lincke, Werner. *Das Stiefmuttermotiv im Märchen der germanischen Völker.* Berlin: Emil Ebering, 1933.

Meletinsky, Eleazer. "Marriage: Its Function and Position in the Structure of Folktales." In *Soviet Structural Folkloristics.* Edited by P. Maranda. The Hague: Mouton, 1974.

Poser, Therese. *Das Volksmärchen: Theorie—Analyse—Didaktik.* Munich: Oldenbourg, 1980.

Propp, Vladimir. "Les transformations des contes fantastiques." In *Théorie de la littérature.* Edited by Tzvetan Todorov. Paris: Editions du Seuil, 1968.

Rank, Otto. *Das Inzest-Motiv in Dichtung und Sage: Grundzüge einer Psychologie des dichterischen Schaffens.* 2d ed. Leipzig: Franz Deuticke, 1926.

Rittershaus, Adeline. *Die neuisländischen Volksmärchen: Ein Beitrag zur vergleichenden Märchenforschung.* Halle a.S.: Max Niemeyer, 1902.

Robert, Marthe, "Un modèle romanesque: Le conte de Grimm." *Preuves* 185 (1966): 24–34.

———. "The Grimm Brothers." *Yale French Studies* 43 (1969): 44–56.

Steig, Reinhold, ed. *Kinder- und Hausmärchen.* Stuttgart: Cotta, 1912.

Stone, Kay. "Things Walt Disney Never Told Us." In *Women and Folklore.* Edited by Claire R. Farrer. Austin: University of Texas Press, 1975.

Weber-Kellermann, Ingeborg. *Die deutsche Familie: Versuch einer Sozialgeschichte.* Frankfurt a.M.: Suhrkamp, 1974.

Wulffen, Erich. "Das Kriminelle im deutschen Volksmärchen." *Archiv für Kriminalistik* 38 (1910): 355.

4   Allegory and the
First School Stories

Samuel Pickering, Jr.

In 1800 Mary Burges published *The Progress of the Pilgrim Good-Intent, in Jacobinical Times*. Believing that liberal educational notions were undermining Britain, she criticized contemporary children's books and lamented the waning popularity of John Bunyan's *The Pilgrim's Progress* (1678). "The pilgrim CHRISTIAN," she wrote, "was the companion of our childhood, till the refinements of modern education banished him from our nurseries." John Locke had convinced the eighteenth century that early education shaped the adult, and Burges's concern over the formative influence of childhood reading upon individuals and ultimately the nation was widespread. Her lament, however, for the disappearance of Bunyan's book was not common. As commercial prosperity created, then enriched, the middle classes in the eighteenth century and as greater numbers of children survived infancy, parents, nurtured on Locke's ideas, envisioned children's futures in secular as well as religious terms. As a result children's books that seemed to promote both moral and worldly success became popular among the expanding middle classes while "godly books" like *The Pilgrim's Progress,* which appeared to denigrate worldly success, gradually lost much of their appeal. Despite the declining popularity of Puritan allegory, however, moral allegory was common at the end of the eighteenth century. If Burges had examined children's literature closely, she would have found several allegorical books specifically indebted to *The Pilgrim's Progress*. Moreover, the allegorical character itself was the most popular character in children's books while the metaphor of the progress, given impetus as well as a new educational direction by Locke, provided the framework of many stories written for children.[1]

In *Some Thoughts Concerning Education* (1693), Locke suggested that learning be made "Play and Recreation" for children. He emphasized uniting amusement with instruction, noting that children could be "cozen'd into a Knowledge of the Letters." Most successful publishers of children's books in the eighteenth century adopted this suggestion. In the introduction to *The History of Tommy Playlove and Jacky Lovebook* (1793), "A Friend" recalled that when he was six he "had a very strong aversion to all kinds of physic." His mother, who was "a mighty good sort of old lady," said to him, "You rogue, you don't know how much good it will do you—it will ease your pain—it will restore you to health." "That may be," the boy answered, but "it is a very disagreeable remedy, and has a most unpleasant taste with it." The boy refused the medicine until an old servant "selected some of the choicest pieces of sweetmeat from a large parcel" and proposed that he eat them immediately after taking the medicine. The boy followed the servant's suggestion; the sweetmeats took away the medicine's bad taste, and A Friend wrote, "I have been since indebted to physic (under the blessing of Heaven) for the preservation of my life." "In like manner," he continued, "as learning is the physic as well as the food of the mind, and as mere instruction is commonly too serious and unentertaining, to be pleasant to every class of readers, I propose to sweeten my instruction (as the old woman took away the disagreeable taste of my physic) by introducing subjects of a pleasanter nature, and occasionally endeavouring to excite an innocent laugh."

Some critics believed that a disproportionate emphasis was put upon amusement in early children's books. In contrast and perhaps as counterbalance to the mixture of amusement and instruction, characters in children's books were often Bunyanesque in their simplicity. With the exception of the individual who was reformed, characters in whose nature virtue and vice were mingled, as amusement and instruction were mingled in the books, rarely appeared. Thus, among the bad companions of Tommy Playlove were Billy Wilful, Bobby Scapegrace, and Ned Slippery, while Peter Pippin's friends in *The History of Little King Pippin* (1814) included Billy Meanwell, Sammy Sober, Bobby Bright, and Tommy Telltruth.[2]

The ancient tradition of linking vices and virtues with animals remained powerful. In Dorothy Kilner's *The History of a Great Many Boys and Girls* (1794), Mary Ann Selfish always "filled her mouth so frightfully full, you cannot think how ugly she looked." Her mother became so exasperated that one day she "took hold of her hand, and said *Mary Ann*! if you will be so like a hog, you shall go and live with the pigs, and not with me and your sisters; for you will teach them to be as bad as yourself. Come, I will carry you to the pigs now, and then you may eat together as fast and as much as you please." Mary Ann cried but her mother was firm and put her in the pigsty. Although it was "a sad thing" for "a little girl to live among the hogs," Dorothy Kilner concluded, "so all greedy children must be treated" (1794, pp. 42–46).

Occasionally allegorical characters were actually transformed into the characters they resembled. In *Vice in its Proper Shape* (1789), a sea captain brought back a "curious little treatise" from the East Indies. The treatise described the sights seen by a man and his seven children. One day while on a walk, they came to a row of small sheds; on a board above the largest shed was written "WAL*KINBE-HOL*DANDLE*ARN, which signifies *Walk in, behold, and learn.*" A Brahmin, named Wiseman, invited them to enter the sheds, saying there were several things to be seen "which might contribute to the entertainment and instruction" of "pretty fellow travellers." Exhibited in the sheds were animals into which the souls of naughty children had transmigrated. In the body of an ass, the children learned, was the soul of Jack Idle. Since early education, Locke taught, made men good or evil, useful or not, it was sad that Jack had not been "a great friend to learning." "His aversion to the useful arts of reading and writing" had been such that he had "an indifferent knowledge of the alphabet" and was "just able to scrawl his own name in characters which were scarcely legible" when he died. One morning as he dawdled on the way to school, Tom Sharper and Dick Lockwit overtook him and persuaded him to play hooky and go fishing. For an hour the boys enjoyed "pretty good sport." Then, Tom's line got entangled in the weeds. Unable to free it himself, he persuaded Jack to attempt to disentangle it by climbing out on a sloping tree, a branch of which hung down over the water above the line. Unfortunately, the branch broke, and Jack, who could not swim, tumbled into the water and drowned.

Among the other animals that Wiseman showed the children was a magpie containing the soul of Dorothy Chatterfast, a monkey with the soul of Monsieur Fribble, a snake containing that of Abigail Eviltongue, and a pig containing that of Anthony Greedyguts. Like poor Jack, Anthony was not a friend to education. He "loved eating much better than reading; and would prefer a tart, a custard, a plum-cake, or even a slice of gingerbread, or an apple, to the prettiest, and most useful little book you could present him with." At eleven he was "such a perfect dunce" that he could scarcely tell his letters. The next year, alas, he ate a dozen penny custards in a single sitting and "thereby gorged his stomach, and threw himself into a mortal fever."[3]

As conductors such as Interpreter and Hopeful helped Christian on his progress, so a character like the Brahmin Wiseman often appeared as a guide in eighteenth-century children's books. In Richard Johnson's *Juvenile Rambles* (c. 1793), for example, Wisdom took Miss Charlotte and Master Billy on an instructive walk through the natural world. The walk ended in a graveyard with Wisdom discussing the deaths of children. Tommy Jones, he explained, jumped into the river to cool off after playing cricket and received such a shock that he was thrown into a fatal fever. When a farmer discovered him robbing his orchard, Dicky Flight tried to escape and fell from a tree, breaking his leg in two places. The break was so severe that Dicky was forced to have his leg "cut off, and he died before it was well" (p. 124).

Adaptations of *The Pilgrim's Progress* appeared in some eighteenth-century children's books. Instead of journeying to heaven and the Celestial City, Master Headstrong and Miss Patient traveled to the Land of Happiness in *The Adventures of Master Headstrong, and Miss Patient* (c. 1802). On setting out for Happiness, Headstrong met three other travelers: Patient, "an elderly staid female called Reason," and Passion, a youth "rushing on like a torrent." Reason volunteered to guide Patient and Headstrong; Patient accepted the offer; but finding the pace too slow, Headstrong ran ahead with Passion. Taking the wrong path, typically, they reached the Palace of False Pleasure, in which "a number of both sexes assembled, dancing, singing, and drinking the most agreeable liquors." At the upper end of the main hall "sat a lady richly habited, of a most excellent shape and complexion, as far as her skin was discovered; but she wore a veil over her face, as if from modesty, and which *Passion* judged to be the thin covering of excellent beauty." Traditionally Passion was unable to discern truth, and instead of being beautiful, the lady was "a most ugly, loathsome witch."

Having forsaken Reason, Headstrong's journey consisted of a series of instructive tribulations. The Palace of False Pleasure led to the "realms of Disappointment," where Headstrong fell into a pit. Reflection helped him out and then told him to avoid "the broad pleasant path that is straight before you and keep the rugged narrow way to the left." Following Reflection's advice, Headstrong caught Reason and Patient, whose plodding pace proved faster than Passion's rush. The adventures contained a wealth of allegorical characters and places: Hope and Fancy, who deluded Headstrong; Experience, who directed him out of a wasteland; Caution, who saved him from the

Cave of Infamy; and Fortitude, who encouraged him to go through "the *bitter water of Repentance*" so that he reached the Temple of Virtue and was able to enter the Land of Happiness with Patient and Reason. Although Headstrong swallowed the black water of repentance, he did not die. Unlike *The Pilgrim's Progress,* which directed pilgrims away from this world, *The Adventures* showed how reasonable and moral behavior helped a person achieve happiness in this life.[4]

In being entirely allegorical *The Adventures* was unusual. In *Some Thoughts,* Locke stressed that children delighted in change and variety and were incapable of paying concentrated attention to any subject, and, as publishers seem to have concluded, any style. Consequently, many early children's books were miscellanies of amusement and instruction as games, stories, fables, riddles, alphabets, maxims, and poetry were jumbled together. Even books that told extended tales were filled with interpolated matter. Usually only a portion of a book was allegorical; before children's attentions wandered, the style of a book often changed. Typically, only part of *The History of Master Jackey and Miss Harriot* (1787) was allegorical. When he was eight years old, Jackey was sent to the village school by his father, Mr. Gracemore, a tradesman. Jackey's cousin Tommy accompanied him. At school, Tommy misbehaved; in contrast Jackey "was so constant in his good behaviour to every body, that the whole village talked of nothing else." The Earl of Fairfame, whose estate was a half-mile outside the village and who was "remarkable for his generosity and benevolence to the poor," eventually heard about Jackey. After Goody Creamer, who supplied him with butter, assured him that Jackey was the best boy in the village, the earl gave Jackey a new watch and invited him and Tommy to visit his estate.

On the boys' arrival Lady Fairfame showed them an allegorical garden—the instructive centerpiece of the book. There were two entrance gates to the garden. The right-hand gate represented the road to virtue and "was planned with the utmost simplicity, or rather rudeness," as cypress hung over it, ivy wrapped around its pillars, and "time seemed to have destroyed all the smoothness and regularity of the stone." Two stone champions with raised clubs guarded the entrance while dragons and serpents "were seen in the most hideous attitudes." Behind the gate the way appeared dark, and only the inscription "*Previous to Virtue*" tempted Jackey and Tommy to enter. In contrast the architecture of the other gate, the road to vice, "was light, elegant, and inviting." Flowers hung about the pillars while "nymphs in the most alluring attitudes beckoned." Over the gate was written "*The descent is easy*" while behind it the path "seemed gay, luxuriant, and capable of affording endless pleasure." Jackey and Tommy entered the garden through this gate. At first the way was pleasing, but soon the sky grew dark, the path became winding, frightful rocks hung over their heads, and eventually they lost their way amid "gloomy caverns, unexpected precipices, awful ruins, heaps of bones, and terrifying sounds." When they were "sufficiently impressed with the horrors of what they heard and saw," Lady Fairfame, now a guide like Wiseman, addressed them, explaining, "My dears, you now see the terrible termination of the road to vice, I would have you learn from what you now see before you, that, *Vice however spacious at its first appearance, terminates in endless misery.*" Then, taking them by the hand, she led them through a hidden door back to the right-hand gate, which they now entered. In a short time, the foreboding entrance was left behind, and they discovered "beautiful cascades, beds of flowers, trees loaded with fruit, and arbours of jessamines and roses." From this little walk, Lady Fairfame said, "you may learn, that, *The Road to virtue terminates in happiness.*"

The allegory ended and Jackey learned well. Unfortunately Tommy, who did not study at school, did not learn his lesson in the garden. Because of her good character, the earl had brought Miss Harriot, a grocer's daughter, to live with him and Lady Fairfame. Tommy eventually became so naughty that without provocation he threw a top at Jackey's head. When Harriot, who was sitting on the side of a wheelbarrow, rebuked him, he pushed her to the ground. The earl saw the incident and sent Tommy home after which he bought Jackey a fine horse. Jackey and Harriot remained with the earl and Lady Fairfame. On his death the earl left them each five hundred pounds. Eight years later Lady Fairfame died and made them "joint heirs to her vast estate." Soon afterward, Mr. Trueman, the earl's former chaplain, married them. In Lady Fairfame's garden Jackey learned lessons which now led him to the rich land of earthly happiness.[5]

The eighteenth-century children's book which made perhaps the best and most interesting use of allegory was *The Prettiest Book for Children; Being The History of the Enchanted Castle; Situated in one of the Fortunate Isles, and governed by the Giant Instruction* (1770). Don Stephano Bunyano, undersecretary to Instruction and "a distant relation of the famous *John Bunyan,*" wrote the *History* while on a journey to England. Mixing amusement with instruction to preach the importance of education, *The Prettiest Book* was a mélange of literary types, smacking of, besides allegory, the Oriental tale, travel books, the fairy tale, and the philosophic story. Wearing a long flowered gown and a hairy cap, waving a white wand, and having a long blue beard, Don Stephano resembled a sorcerer. In his habits he was more conventional, and despite his clothes and beard he behaved like a good little boy. As soon as he got up in the morning, he said his prayers, washed his face and hands, and combed his beard. Instruction was also exotic in appearance. He was ten feet tall and had a gold beard and gold hair which hung down over his shoulders "in flowing ringlets." On his head he wore a green turban ornamented with gold and diamonds while about his middle he wore a purple vest embroidered with pearls. He was so handsome, Don Stephano declared, that "if some of your English ladies were to see him, they would either wish that he was reduced to the common size, or that they themselves were born *giantesses*." Despite his Oriental appearance, however, there was no taint of the lascivious Levant about Instruction. He was a moral giant, and English ladies would have found him disappointing. He believed the Bible was the best book in the world and said his prayers every morning and every evening. Instead of a doe-eyed houri, his wife was Lady Good-Example and his five daughters were named Piety, Patience, Charity, Sobriety, and Prudence.

With his amusing personality and colorful dress Don Stephano was Bunyan adapted to the world of the eighteenth-century children's book. *The Prettiest Book* tried to make its brightened allegory more appealing to contemporary children. The Enchanted Castle was located on "the *seat of education*," the smallest of the Fortunate Isles. In its decorous symmetry, the castle was an emblem of education. It formed a perfect square, each of its walls being eighty yards long. In the middle was "a spacious and beautiful court" paved with stone. In the center a fountain cast up "water as pure as crystal, to a most surprising height." Several tutors, supported by Instruction, lived in the castle, and the children of the rich and the poor—the latter if they passed an examination—traveled "hither to be educated" from the other Fortunate Isles. Locke's educational theories were democratizing. If education and the hard work it involved, not the accident of birth, determined a child's future and his worth, then social hierarchies, structured primarily on birth, were raised on a false basis. Those children and parents who judged people on the basis of birth or inherited position and thereby ignored the importance of childhood education resembled Bunyan's affluent sinners, so trapped by the superficial surface of things that they slighted essential Christian teaching. As such sinners could not enter the Celestial City, so Instruction refused entry to the Enchanted Castle to wicked children who believed that birth, not education and its result, right behavior, made the man. Instruction believed, Don Stephano wrote, "that no man can be so great, or so rich and powerful, as to have any right to excuse himself from his duty. Some little boys, indeed, because they are gentlemens sons, and are finely dressed, and eat and drink, as we say, of the best of every thing, are silly enough to think that they may do all manner of wickedness and mischief. But these are very stupid and naughty children; and if they were even to set their feet in the *Enchanted Castle*, or even to come near to the door of it, the good giant would spurn them out of his sight, or perhaps do something worse with them."

In the castle great stress was put upon proper learning, the primary manifestation of which was good behavior. The porter of the castle, Mr. Alphabet, refused entrance to bad children and to ignorant children, who because right education shaped the good adult were certain to be bad. If a child did not know his letters, Mr. Alphabet sent "him packing like a dunce and a blockhead." After being admitted to the castle, children came to the Picture Gallery, where Mr. Interpreter met them. The gallery's collection consisted entirely of instructive pictures and contained Mr. Dutiful's depiction of the death of Absalom, Mr. Good's painting of the parable of the cruel steward, and Mr. Mannerly's picture of "foaming bears" pursuing the children who mocked Elisha. After visiting the gallery, children went to the museum, where Mr. Set'em-right, the caretaker, exhibited such curiosities as the Moneycup, which turned all money placed in it to dust and thus taught "the real value of your money,"and the twelve-foot-long spy glass made by Mr. Faith-and-hope, through which children could glimpse "a noble city" in comparison to which the Enchanted Castle was but "a fool." Beyond the museum lay the library; over the door in the language of the Isles was inscribed, "THEF EAROF THELOR DIS THEBE GINING OFWIS DOM, and means in English, The Fear of the Lord is the Begining of Wisdom."

Instruction met the children in the library and presented each a "neat Bible." At the beginning of *The Prettiest Book*, Don Stephano criticized children's books. Petty writers, he wrote, "stuffed their little books with so many out-of-the-way expressions, and so many words which are borrowed from the learned and other languages" that the insides of many books "were as fine and tawdry as the gilt paper on the coverlids." As a result such books did not teach children "plain good sense" but "only taught them to talk *gibberish*." Allegory at its best encouraged children to look beyond appearances: so Instruction, like Don Stephano, did not want glittering words to distract children from the path of right education. Inside the library the giant showed children a parrot, who could read and talk and "was no stranger to Greek and Latin." Unfortunately, the parrot could not comprehend meaning. "Such Parrots," Don Stephano wrote, were "to be met with in many a fine library in England." "I hope, however," he added, "that all my little readers, when they take a book into their hands, will be resolved to understand it as they go along."

In the library reading for understanding, and thereby being educated for practical life, was emphasized. On the door leading out of the library was a picture of "a tall, meagre, lanthorn-jawed, hollow-eyed, raw-boned fellow, who has his mouth as full of victuals as he can cram it, with a large piece of flesh in each hand, and the greatest plenty of all manner of provisions around him." The picture was an allegorical representation of the *"Book-glutton,"* the "person who reads every thing, and remembers nothing."[6]

Although the picture of the Book-glutton was striking, like the other allegorical furnishings of the Enchanted Castle, it smacked heavily of the ingenious. If education, of which childhood reading was a significant part, did determine success, then allegorical ingenuity, like the alluring labyrinth in Lady Fairfame's garden in which Jackey and Tommy lost their way, could mislead young readers. As the parrot read but did not understand, so the decorative surface of allegory could so interest children that they would miss a book's homey educational lessons. Burges's "modern education" did not banish allegory as it did Christian. But the desire for an education that would enable children to be successful in the modern world contributed to the popularity of the school story, a form that often taught the same educational lessons as allegory and depended upon similar literary devices but whose "story" occurred in a seemingly more realistic, less distracting landscape. The similarity between allegory and early school stories was great. By transforming the Enchanted Castle, for example, into a school and the giant Instruction into a schoolmaster, *The Prettiest Book* almost became a school story. The children's educational progress through the various rooms of the castle then would become a progress through forms and beyond various temptations.

In contrast to conventional allegory, which appeared a world apart, the school story appeared as a recognizable, albeit diminutive, world. "A school may be styled," the author of *The School-Fellows* (1818) wrote, "the world in miniature." As Christian left the City of Destruction and began a spiritual progress toward eternal life, so the schoolboy left the protecting, and confining, family to begin an educational progress through life. The boy, Ellenor Fenn wrote in *School Dialogues for Boys* (1783), emerged from under his mother's "wing into that LITTLE WORLD, a SCHOOL." Although this little world seemed more realistic than that of allegory, the characters which inhabited it were generally allegorical. In Sarah Fielding's *The Governess* (1749), the first school story in children's literature, among Mrs. Teachum's pupils were Dolly Friendly, Lucy Sly, Nanny Spruce, Henny Fret, and Jenny Peace. Among *The Little Female Orators* (1770) at boarding school were Dolly Goodchild, Betsy Thoughtful,

Deborah Mindful, and Sally Readwell, while attending Mrs. Propriety's class in *The Village School* (1817) were Kate Saucy, Bet Dirty, Ned Rattle, Sukey Giddy, and Charles Mindbook. In *School Dialogues for Boys,* Mr. Aweful the master, Mr. Wiseman the usher, and Mr. Sage the assistant taught a range of students including Candid, Sensible, Worthy, Spiteful, Meek, Pert, Flaunt, Frisk, Easy, Tinsel, Flippant, Subtle, Mildmay, and Chatter.[7]

As Christian denied the tempting byways of the world in order to follow "the Road" to the Celestial City, so learning to say *no* was a student's first lesson. "The first thing necessary for a boy to learn, at going to a great school," Sensible informed Sprightly on his arrival at Mr. Aweful's school, "is to be able to say, NO, with a firm and manly assurance." Impulsive behavior like that of Master Headstrong led students astray. "If we accustom ourselves to act without consideration in *trifles,*" Mr. Rotchford told Charles in *The Rotchfords* (c. 1783), "it will not be long before we shall proceed upon the same sandy foundation to commit actions of the greatest importance." Since, as Locke taught, early impressions—and thus from the eighteenth century's perspective, actions—had lasting consequences, turning from the entrapping sands to that road built upon a firm educational foundation was difficult. Unlike Christian, who lived only for the next world and sought only the approval of God, schoolchildren were educated for this world. As a result they frequently confused popularity with success and erred through the desire to please. In *School Occurrences* (1782) Miss Greedy refused to share a cake which she had received from home and instead locked it in her bureau. When Greedy left the room, Miss Pry suggested to the other students that they open the bureau and eat the cake before it spoiled. Several girls tried their keys in Greedy's bureau with no success; then Pry recalled that Miss Sprightly's key opened the bureau. At first Sprightly refused to give the girls her key, but under pressure she lost, as she said, "the right way" and gave them her key. Before the cake was divided, however, she struggled and, regaining her way, refused a piece. Although her schoolmates accused her of being "squeamish, and affectedly scrupulous," she responded that she "regretted nothing but that she had not had sufficient resolution to persist in her refusal of the key."[8]

More dangerous to resolution than scorn was the higher-caliber ridicule, "the most dangerous weapon," Hannah More wrote, "in the whole arsenal of impiety." In school stories, educational and moral virtues were entwined, and the child who could not resist being ridiculed out of his faith was too weak to make educational progress. "When I knelt down the first night to say my prayers," Supple, a new student at Mr. Aweful's, recounted of a former school, "they called out, '*a Methodist!*' " "What did you do?" Sprightly asked. "I never durst kneel any more, for shame," Supple replied, adding that he knew he "was doing ill, yet had not the courage to brave the jests of my naughty companions." "Be as compliant as you please in things indifferent," said Sensible, who overheard the conversation and who had served as Sprightly's guide; "let others choose whether you shall drive a hoop, or play at leap-frog;—but where *right* and *wrong* are concerned, be *firm.*"[9]

Children's books like *The Adventures of Master Headstrong* and *The Prettiest Book,* in which allegory taught only general moral and educational truths, appealed to boys and girls alike. In contrast school stories were usually written for either boys or girls but not for both. In part the differentiation simply mirrored contemporary education in which boys and girls above the lower classes attended separate schools. In part, however, it reflected the age's strong belief in the formative influence of childhood reading. Since the success and ways of behavior thought proper for men were not the same as those considered proper for women, children's books, and in particular school stories that concentrated upon education, often described an educational progress for boys different from that for girls. The difference between books written for girls and for boys was especially great in attitudes toward firmness. With the exception of books written for lower-class boys, which often viewed fighting as socially disruptive and instead taught the passive virtues of humility and resignation, school stories for boys frequently included a fight. By the end of the eighteenth century, most children's books stripped Christianity of particular doctrine, leaving it a faith of general morality and good deeds. As a consequence, although fights in school stories harkened back in part to Christian's lonely struggle with Apollyon, they also looked forward to Kingsley's muscular Christianity in which the true believer fought not simply in the Valley of Humiliation for his own soul but in the social area as the champion of the weak and oppressed.

The overwhelming majority of early children's books were written for the middle classes and thus appealed to their aspirations. The foes against which the heroes of the first school stories struggled were usually aristocratic. Because its wealth and position were inherited, the very existence of an aristocracy denied what Locke taught and the middle classes believed: that education determined a person's moral, economic, and finally social success. In an ideal educational world, no man would inherit prestige or power, he would be educated for it. Achieving the right education and consequently position depended upon work not privilege. In such an educational world, there was no place for an aristocracy, and in school stories, hard-working, middle-class boys thrashed aristocrats, in the process either driving them out of school or converting them to belief in the crucial importance of education. Even when they were not allegorical, the names of students involved in fights in school stories usually revealed their social classes and thereby their characters. In *Tales of the Academy* (1820), the two leading pupils in Mr. Osgood's school in the village of Muchlore were Adolphus and Ernest. Although born with "most genius," Adolphus, resting on his inheritance, neglected his education and as a result Ernest excelled him first in studies and then, because of his work, in morality.

Although Mr. Osgood did not approve, fagging existed in his school. One Saturday after the boys received their weekly pocket money, Ernest saw one of Adolphus's fags crying and discovered that Adolphus had taken the boy's money and given it to another fag to buy apples. "I suppose you owed him the money," Ernest said. "No," the boy answered; "he told me I *must* lend it to him; and because I wouldn't lend it, he said he would take it, and pay me at the half-year's end (in the language of the academy, not at all)." Although interfering with another's fag went against custom, Ernest, as a middle-class champion, had been educated to support decency, and he retrieved the boy's money from the gardener selling apples. When Adolphus appeared, Ernest told him his apples were still with the gardener, adding, "If you want them, find some more honest means to obtain them." Like Apollyon before Christian, Adolphus behaved histrionically. He turned pale; his lips quivered with rage, and he "fiercely enquired what Ernest meant by interfering between him and his fag." "To rescue the little one from your injustice and oppression," Ernest answered, "calmly, but firmly." "Secretly fearing" Ernest, as a portion of the aristocracy feared the leveling effects of education, "but not knowing how to vent his growing rage," Adolphus aimed "a blow at his little fag, who still stood trembling by." By offering both the opportunity to better their lots in life, education emblematically joined the lower and comparatively weak and the middle and comparatively strong classes; symbolically, Ernest stuck his arm out and "received the blow, casting a glance of contempt at Adolphus." Then, facing the little boy, Ernest assured him that he would protect him from oppression in the future. While Ernest was turned away from him, Adolphus hit him. Ernest, however, was unhurt and, grabbing Adolphus by his shoulders, "laid him without the effort of a blow, at his length upon the ground."

Adolphus was stunned, and although "hootings and other sounds expressive of contempt" assailed him, he refused to fight longer and "took to his heels, and was not seen again by his school-companions during the day." In fleeing the punishment he deserved, Adolphus refused to struggle with his weakness, and straying far from the road to virtue and success, thereby began a sad demonic wandering. After he returned to school, he plotted against Ernest under the cover of professed friendship. Craftily, he spilled ink across Ernest's copybook, and like the snake spoiling Eden, poisoned Ernest's prize rosebush and opened a fence and let pigs into his garden. Eventually, however, his deeds were found out, and he was expelled. He became addicted to vice, and after losing his inheritance gambling, became a highwayman. When last heard from, he was imprisoned in the hulk *Retribution*. "I had become a pest and a disgrace," he wrote, "THROUGH THOSE ROOTED HABITS OF CRAFTINESS AND DUPLICITY I ALLOWED TO BECOME MY MASTERS IN MY BOYHOOD."[10]

In emphasizing the importance of education for this world, there was the danger of teaching children to overvalue worldly things and worldly behavior. If education, Hannah More wrote, was "a school to fit us for life," then, she reminded readers, life was "a school to fit us for eternity" (1799, 1:56–57). In part aristocrats were villains in school fights because they represented the corrupting influence of luxury. At the end of the eighteenth century, social critics conventionally blamed the aristocracy for undermining the morality of the middle classes, arguing that the upper classes set poor standards for emulation by living in a luxurious fashion. "The seeds of false-refinement," Mary Wollstonecraft wrote, "undermine the very foundation of virtue and spread corruption through the whole mass of society" (1792, p. 5).

Not only did aristocrats suffer beatings as emblems of luxury in school stories, but numerous children's books also described the errors of parents who aped luxurious behavior and gave their children educations that schooled them for neither life nor eternity. *The History of Jacky Idle and Dickey Diligent* (1806) described the unfortunate effects of, as Jane West put it in *Letters to a Young Lady* (1806), the "rapid increase of wealth to families that have not, either by habit or education, been taught the proper use of it" (1:139). Jacky Idle was the son of a tradesman who, having inherited a fortune from a relative, quit the solid middle-class world in which he belonged, and, moving from the city to the country, adopted a style of living which he thought aristocratic. Believing that money not education made the man, he paid little attention to his son's studies and allowed him to be spoiled by his wife. When Jacky eventually went to school, Mrs. Idle warned the master "never to chastise him, nor even to force him to learn any thing against his inclination," observing "that a depth of education was necessary only to those who were hereafter obliged to work for their labour." As a result of this injunction, which stressed inheritance rather than education, Jacky never began a proper educational progress and, like Adolphus who fled hardship, was doomed to wander from virtue and success.

Attending school with Jacky was Dickey Diligent, who because his parents were poor, realized the importance of education. During the holidays, Dickey visited Jacky and found a home resembling a children's book in which there was an imbalance between amusement and instruction. When Jacky arrived home, Mrs. Idle "loaded her son's stomach with cakes and sweetmeats." As sweets killed Anthony Greedyguts, so Jacky "grew dull and pale, and soon afterwards sick indeed." Instead of feeding her son the plain provender of a good education on his recovery, Mrs. Idle gave him a party and, inviting the "neighboring gentry and people of fashion," exposed him to debilitating fare. During the party an old lady exclaimed, "What a pity it is that such a smart young gentleman, as is master Jacky, should spoil his fine eyes by reading, and hurt his stomach by pressing against a desk while writing. Gentlemen of fortune have no business with the sciences; they should be left to the labour of poor people." Although Dickey Diligent remained silent, his face revealed his thoughts, and Mr. Freeport, a wealthy merchant sitting nearby, asked him if he disagreed. "I do not know how to answer you, sir," Dickey replied, "for the old lady must certainly know better than I." The answer satisfied Freeport, and he offered the boy a position as clerk in his countinghouse. Dickey's diligence brought rewards; after some years, he became Freeport's partner and married his only daughter.

In contrast Jacky, whose education had not prepared him to progress through life, did poorly. After receiving his inheritance, he "launched out on the dangerous ocean of the wide world, without any compass to steer by, without the least ballast to keep his vessel steady, and without any knowledge to direct the helm." As a consequence, sharpers stripped him of his money, then, like Mary Ann Selfish's mother, put him with suitable companions, advising him to "return to the country, and there get your living by looking after hogs, sheep, and other castle." On discovering him living in poverty, Dickey came to Jacky's aid. Since character and success, however, were determined by early education, Idle was "totally incapable of undertaking" and "too indolent to attend to any kind of employment." Consequently, he lived as a pensioner on Diligent's bounty "until ease and indolence," signs of degeneracy often associated with aristocracy, "brought on a complication of disorders, which terminated in death."[11]

Fighting in school stories written primarily for girls differed from that in books for boys. In the latter, fights usually represented an allegorical struggle between good and evil; on the level of the individual the fights marked passing through a stage in development in which the rightly educated boy proved himself firm enough to overcome obstacles and worthy of continuing his progress toward success. In books for girls physical struggles rarely occurred between individuals; instead fights represented the general breakdown of social order, since the domestic and "passive virtues" that women ideally embodied bound society together. Although women were not entitled to places in Parliament, they were, Jane West wrote, "*legislators* in the most important sense of the word" (1806, 1: 58, 121). The home was a microcosm of the nation and was the "proper sphere" for women, Mrs. Taylor wrote in *A Correspondence between a Mother and Her Daughter at School* (1817). Although men had "much to do with the world without" and "our field of action" was circumscribed, she declared, women who discharged their duties at home "may produce effects equally beneficial and extensive" (pp. 140–41).

The first school story, *The Governess*, began with a fight that revealed the emphasis placed upon the influence of education in eighteenth-century children's books. Mrs. Teachum gave a basket of apples to her senior girl Jenny Peace to distribute among her schoolmates. One apple was bigger than the rest, and although Jenny parceled the apples out as fairly as possible, all the girls coveted the large apple and began to quarrel. To quiet them, Jenny offered to divide it. When this failed to halt the bickering, Jenny threw the apple over a hedge. Even this did not restore calm, and a general fray erupted as the girls fought over who should have had the right to the apple. As desire for apple led to the expulsion of those first children, Adam and Eve, from Eden, so it introduced discord into the school world. In contrast to the Bible and *The Pilgrim's Progress*, however, education, not right religion, now restored harmony to life. Although education and religion were closely linked (Mrs. Teachum was the widow of a clergyman), they were nevertheless separate, for not God or a minister, but Mrs. Teachum instructed the children "in all proper Forms of Behaviour." No other fights occurred in *The Governess*. Having curbed the outbreak of original temper, if not sin, Mrs. Teachum directed her pupils' progresses so that they would enjoy successful lives and be "obedient to their superiors, and gentle, kind, and affectionate to each other" (Fielding, 1749, pp. 1–2).

In school stories for girls, great emphasis was put upon the passive virtues, "fortitude, temperance, meekness, faith, and self-denial," as Hannah More listed them (1799, 1:149–50). Instead of fighting an individual to overcome a symbolic obstacle, girls were taught to conquer the urge to fight. "The regulation of the temper," Priscilla Wakefield wrote in *Reflections on the Present Condition of the*

Female Sex (1798), "is of all qualities the most useful to conduct us steadily through vexatious circumstances" (p. 34). In contrast, regulation of the temper did not always overcome evil in boys' books, and good boys often fought out of a sense of virtuous indignation. In *The Disgraceful Effects of Falsehood* (1807), Henry Cathcart "was as much beloved for the sweetness of his temper, as he was admired for that spirit which would not suffer the *defenceless* to be *oppressed*." When he returned to school after an illness and learned that Adolphus Fitzhue had abused his brother Edward, a fag, "the fire of indignation sparkled in his eyes, and without even replying to the account which had been communicated, he immediately hastened to Fitzhue's room." There, despite Fitzhue's basing his defense upon passivity, saying he was "rather too much of a *gentleman* to *fight*," Cathcart grabbed him by the collar and thrashed him "with all his strength" (Pilkington, 1807, pp. 96–102). In *Anecdotes of a Boarding-School* (1795), a girls' story in which wrongdoing provoked Martha Beauchamp, like Henry Cathcart, to lose her temper, the attitude toward fighting was very different. Ever since Martha entered Mrs. Steward's school, some of her classmates, including Miss Grumpton, Miss Sneak, Miss Lapwing, and Miss Stone, ridiculed her good manners and religion. When Martha asked her mother how she should behave, Mrs. Beauchamp wrote, "Gentleness and forbearance should at all times be the characteristics of a young lady's conduct, even to those who offend her." Following her mother's advice, Martha tried to ignore her persecutors until one day Miss Grumpton crept behind her and snatched a letter from Mrs. Beauchamp out of her hand. When Martha tried to retrieve the letter, the bad girls passed it about the room. Martha became frantic, and, losing her temper, tore half a yard of binding from Miss Grumpton's shirt. A fight began, and soon all the girls in the room were involved. Hearing the commotion, Mrs. Steward rushed in and found Martha "endeavouring to bite the hands of a Miss *Fangly*, a great girl, who was holding her by the arms to prevent her going to her letter, and at the same time, making the most use she could of her feet, to induce her to set her at liberty." Instead of being transformed into a righteous champion like Henry Cathcart, Martha's loss of temper, albeit understandable, turned her and her schoolmates into animals. "My dear," Mrs. Steward told her, "though offended, we are not to suffer our passions to transport us beyond all bounds, and permit ourselves to kick and bite like dogs, who have no understanding or reason to guide them" (Kilner, 1795, pp. 52–64).

In school stories for girls, the emphasis put upon controlling the passions usually turned potential conflicts with external opponents into internal struggles. Because it encouraged rivalries that could grow heated and develop into open conflicts, competition was frequently discouraged. Mrs. W., her governess, Laura wrote in *Correspondence between a Mother and Her Daughter at School,* "takes great pains to check in us a spirit of competition and rivalry; while she endeavors to inspire us with the genuine love of knowledge, and with a true taste for our acquirements; urging us to be more ambitious to excel *ourselves* than to excel each other" (Taylor and Taylor, 1817, pp. 12–13). In Maria Edgeworth's story "The Bracelets" (1800), Mrs. Villars awarded a prize "for successful application" at the end of each school year. The two leading candidates were Cecila and Leonora. After her mother's death, Cecila was raised by her father. Although he attempted to fill a mother's role "in the best and kindest manner, he had insensibly infused into his daughter's mind a portion of that enterprizing, independent spirit, which he justly deemed essential to the character of her brother." As a result Cecila's virtues "were more estimable in a man, than desirable in a woman." In contrast Leonora, who had been reared by a mother, "had a character and virtues, more peculiar to a female." Her judgment, Maria Edgeworth wrote, "had been early cultivated, and her good sense employed in the regulation of her conduct; she had been habituated to that restraint, which, as a woman, she was to expect in life, and early accustomed to yield." Since she had been raised practically as a boy, Cecila delighted in competition and won the prize for application. Success, however, did not benefit her character or bring lasting satisfaction. As soon as she received the award, Cecila ran exulting like a boy down a flight of stairs and knocked over little Louisa, breaking a china doll that Louisa had just received from her mother. As the doll broke easily, so Cecila's happiness, built not upon solid feminine restraint but upon a denatured masculine enjoyment of competition, shattered quickly. Cecila laughed when she broke the doll and was rebuked by Leonora. Cecila was unhappy from this moment until she won an inner struggle and, controlling her ambition and "spirit of competition," cast a vote she thought would break a tie between Leonora and herself and give Leonora an award for "most amiable."[12]

Inner struggles "to excel" a selfish or ambitious self provided the substance of most fights in school stories for girls. For the most part, the battle against, as Jane West put it, "this insatiable monster, a rage for distinction" appeared as a personal struggle against vanity and the superficial attractions of aristocratic luxury (1806, 1: 145). The "phrenzy of accomplishments," Hannah More wrote, "is no longer restricted within the usual limits of rank and fortune; the middle orders have caught the contagion, and it rages with increasing violence" (1799, p. 62). In early children's books, vanity and luxurious living were responsible for the deaths of many children like Jacky Idle. Curing the contagion was difficult and in books for girls depended upon an education that would create immunity to luxury. Written primarily for the middle classes, early children's books not only preached the danger of living luxuriously but also taught that if girls from families of rank and fortune received proper educations they would reject luxury and, embracing the passive virtues of temperance and self-denial, would become true aristocrats, in effect spiritual and moral members of the middle class. In *The Mother's Gift* (1787) Mrs. Forbes sent her niece Harriet to Mrs. Lawes's school, apologizing that the girl had "the Misfortune" of being "a person of Quality." Although Harriet had "been taught the Accomplishments that make a Figure in the World" and could sing, dance, play the harpsichord, and understand "every Form of good Breeding," she was "entirely deficient in every Part of useful Knowledge" and "ignorant of the Duties which are the Improvement of Life." After a struggle with herself, similar to that of Cecila, Harriet overcame vanity. Instead of remaining merely a figure, or the sum of worldly accomplishments, she grew into a substantial person. She received a proper education and so progressed that she recognized her duties and led a useful, benevolent life. "All who are acquainted with her," the author wrote, "had Reason to bless the Time when the wild Shoots of Pride and Extravagance were pruned, and the Buds of Virtue and Religion grafted on her Heart."[13]

Since "the sphere of feminine action," Priscilla Wakefield wrote, "is contracted by numberless difficulties, that are no impediments to masculine exertions" and fights in school stories for girls were more internal than external, Harriet would use her knowledge and exercise her duties more in the domestic than in the public world (1798, p. 9). Although boys, unlike Harriet, would eventually have "much to do with the world without," nevertheless the progresses of both boys and girls in school stories were confined to a comparatively limited landscape. As Christian had to hold fast to religion and remain on "the Road" to reach the Celestial City, so children's books discouraged students from prematurely wandering beyond school into the wider world where they could be distracted from proper education. Making educational progress was difficult, and students who ran away from school usually were either bad or weak. *The Adventures of Timothy Thoughtless* (1813) described the sufferings of a small boy who fled boarding school. Timothy was the son of a confectioner who "by his own industry and attention to business" became wealthy. Although Mr. Thoughtless, unlike Jacky Idle's parents, did not ape the aristocracy, his son was spoiled literally and metaphorically by indulging in the insubstantial sweets made possible by wealth. After Timothy became sickly, Mr. Thoughtless sent him to Greengrove House, a boarding school. Instead of dining on luxurious "sweet articles," students ate hearty meals, and Timothy soon grew both healthy and "forward in his learning."

Timothy spent two happy years at the school; then, inevitably, Will Grumble, who had been expelled from other schools, appeared in the green grove. Like the serpent in Eden or the apple in Mrs. Teachum's school, Grumble brought discord. "His joy was to tell one boy that Master Such-a-one had said different falsities of him, and then he would go to the other with similar lies, till he had produced a quarrel or a boxing match." When the rest of the boys were at play, he crept into the schoolroom and blotted copybooks. Like Adolphus in *Tales of the Academy,* he destroyed gardens, pulling up flowers and breaking fences. Because of his "crimes," innocent boys were flogged. He criticized the school and the master, Mr. Stubbs, so cleverly that students "began to think themselves very badly used, and became discontented, careless, and refractory." As a consequence, Mrs. Stubbs became more severe and unhappiness spread. One day Grumble stole a book from Master White's playbox. When asked about it, he, like every other boy in school, denied knowledge of the theft. A week later, "as Timothy was watching a large snail crawling up the wall of the barn, which was old and full of chinks," he discovered the book hidden between two bricks. Mr. Stubbs, who was on his way to the stables, saw Timothy take the book from the wall and concluded he had stolen it from Master White. So great was his anger "at finding a thief in one of his scholars, as he supposed," Stubbs did not listen to Timothy's explanation and instead beat him severely with his riding whip and declared he would flog him the next morning before the entire school.

Timothy decided to write his father, but Grumble, who had witnessed his beating and said nothing, persuaded him to run away from school with him. The next morning Timothy fled with Grumble, but like Headstrong in the company of Passion, soon found the way difficult and became lost. In leaving school and thereby the education that determined both moral and economic success, Timothy practically condemned himself, like those who took the wrong gate in Lady Fairfame's garden, to *"endless misery."* At times the landscape through which he and Grumble wandered resembled Hell. Exhausted, the two boys eventually fell asleep, only to be awakened by a storm. "The lightening flashed as if all the heavens were on fire, and the thunder shook the ground where they stood with its dreadful explosions; the wind bent the branches of the trees in the hedges, mingling its loud howlings with the thunder; and the rain, rushed down upon them in torrents." To escape the rain, Grumble took shelter under a beech. Unfortunately, just as he reached the tree, "a prodigious limb, torn off by a sudden gust of wind, fell upon him with a frightful crash, dashing out his brains upon the spot." In undermining his and other boys' educations, Grumble had earlier destroyed all possibilities for positive development, and his early death, like that of Jacky Idle, was fortunate and inevitable. "Thus ended," Walker wrote, "the life of that wicked boy, who, had Providence suffered him to live, would in all probability have grown up in wickedness, till some of his actions would have brought him to the gallows."

Since early impressions and actions had lasting consequences, finding one's way back to school or to the right educational road was not easy. Education taught control and discipline, and as uneducated Grumble had, in a sense, been at the mercy of his evil impulses, so Timothy, who had rashly rejected education, was now at the mercy of unrestrained elements within society. After being chased and bitten by dogs, he eventually fell asleep again, this time to be "suddenly awakened by someone pinching his cheek" almost like a witch seeing if her victim were fat enough for the oven. Timothy was horrified to find "a beggar woman stooping above him. Her face was haggard, and withered, and frightfully marked with small-pox." She wore rags and on her back was a filthy child. Beside her stood Teddy, a boy Timothy's own age, without hat, shoes, or stockings. "Pray, don't kill me!" Timothy cried in terror. "What money have you got, you little thief?" the woman answered, ordering Teddy to search him. Timothy's money did not satisfy Teddy, and after taking his hat, hankerchief, and knife, he said, "I think, mother, I should like his shoes." " 'Oh, what shall I do? what shall I do?' cried Tim, in a grievous tone of voice; 'Oh, that I had never left Mr. Stubbs.' "

"Give over your piping and snivelling," the woman cried, and cursing, added, "or I'll be after stripping your carcase, and murdering you.—Come, pull off this green jacket and trowsers, and change cloaths with the lad." In running away from school, Timothy had unconsciously turned away from education, which, children's books taught, was primarily responsible for the differences among men. Without an education, Timothy was doomed to be a Teddy, and after the beggar woman left, he wandered aimlessly. Instead of making an educational progress during which he gradually disciplined himself and thus asserted control over circumstances, he became the pawn of circumstances and the emblem of the uneducated man. He joined a group of potters headed for a fair. When they deserted him, a vagrant fiddler and ballad singer made him beg. Only luck saved him from being murdered or becoming a thief. For a while, he lived in a poorhouse; then he was apprenticed to Sam Sturdy, a master chimney sweep. Eventually he obtained a piece of paper, and because he remembered his letters wrote his parents, who rescued him and sent him, repentant, back to Greengrove House. "Had you waited," his father scolded him, "your innocence would shortly have appeared, and your character would have been redeemed."[14]

Unlike an educational progress, Timothy's undisciplined wanderings did not bring knowledge or enable him to cope better with life. He learned only that he wanted to return to school. As Christian had to remain on the Road to reach the Celestial City, so Timothy had to stay in school in order to succeed in life. In school stories, the child who became good quickly learned, as Sensible informed Sprightly, to say *no*. Outside school, life was anarchic and instead of controlling circumstance by saying *no*, the child was more or less controlled by circumstances; instead of growing by denying experience, he was ruined by experiencing. However, just as the middle classes in the eighteenth century generally believed that Bunyan's emphasis upon religion narrowly limited a child's educational progress, a small but significant and growing number of writers and critics held that attitudes like those in school stories which confined children to the world within schools were unnaturally constricting and ultimately undermined education and development. Experience in its gothic multiplicity, Rousseau argued, taught better than the giant Instruction in his neoclassical Enchanted, and thereby false, Castle. "All things," Rousseau wrote in *Emilius and Sophia* (1762–63), "are as good as their Creator made them, but every thing degenerates in the hands of man. By human art is our native soil compelled to nourish exotic plants, and one tree to bear the fruits of another. Improving man makes a general confusion of elements, climates, and seasons: he mutilates his dogs, his horses, and his slaves: he defaces, he confounds every thing, as if he delighted in nothing but monsters and deformity" (1: 1–2). Even more than the natural world, improving or educating man mutilated human nature, and *Emilius* taught the importance of learning through experience rather than instruction. Experiences like those Timothy Thoughtless endured would not have incapacitated Emilius but would have made him more capable. Necessity, Joachim Campe argued in *The New Robinson Crusoe* (1790), "is the mother of invention. She teaches us many things which we should not know but for her" (p. 45). In book 5 of *The Prelude* (1805 version), Wordsworth celebrated what he called "a race of real children" and criticized educators who attempted to shape adults by confining children "like engines" to a proper instructive road. Instead, he believed, children should roam freely across "the open ground of fancy" (pp. 73–79). As their worlds expanded, so would their capacities and—unlike engines, who would be knocked spinning off the road by unusual events—real children would be able to cope with the unexpected. An education which only taught girls "all proper Forms of Behaviour" and which emphasized discipline, preaching control of the passions as Mrs. Steward did to Martha Beauchamp, was partly responsible, Mary Wollstonecraft argued, for making women inferior to men. "The regulation of the passions," she wrote, "is not always, wisdom. On the contrary, it should seem that one reason why men have superior judgment, and more fortitude than women, is undoubtedly this, that they give a freer scope to the grand passions, and by more frequently going astray enlarge their minds" (1792, p. 246).

In this attitude was the lineage of different kinds of heroes for children's books: for example, the boy who transgressed against convention and appeared bad but was actually good, and the vagabond who made no educational progress and seemed to be drifting aimlessly but who was rapidly developing his capacities to cope with and succeed in life. The characters offered enormous possibilities. For those who believed that society and its institutions were corrupt and that education perpetrated social evil, the character became the voice of truth or nature, which, in fact, were often the same. Thus uneducated children were transfomed into infant philosophers while the Teddys of the road, Kim and Huck, were turned into teachers and social scientists. Because such a character's growth depended upon challenging experiences, he was often the hero of a picaresque story. Except for furnishing the foil of the moment, the school world was too limited for the character's development. Moreover, because belief in the healthy, formative influence of an educational progress was widespread when the first school stories were published, if such a character attended a school, he usually appeared as a demonic, corrupting Grumble or, more good-humoredly, as simply misled.[15]

Robinson Crusoe was the first book Emilius read. Stripped of religious fervor, it became symbolic educational writ for people like Rousseau, who believed that a child "should receive no kind" of instruction "but from experience" (1762, 1: 132). In school stories a Robinson Crusoe-like student occasionally appeared; his independent wanderings, however, did not create self-sufficiency; instead experience usually proved unmanageably disruptive and drove him from the fields and woods back to the schoolroom, where he joined classmates in a conventional educational progress. In *Tales of the Academy* Paul attended Mr. Osgood's school in the village of Muchlore. "Of all the remarkable characters of whom he had ever read, whether kings, conquerors, heroes, statesmen, philosophers, poets, or sages, he neither envied the success, the splendor, the glory, nor the wisdom: his sage, his philosopher, his hero, his king was—Robinson Crusoe." During his free time Paul delighted in wandering alone through the woods that surrounded Muchlore or along the banks of a nearby river. "The common forms of society . . . its habits, ceremonies, and established usages, appeared to him but so many bars to the felicity which, he was persuaded the recluse must enjoy without hindrance or molestation." In the school yard he built a hut and furnished it with a three-legged table, after which he entertained classmates, serving them homemade wine. Echoing Rousseau, he frequently lamented "that such institutions as academies should ever have been allowed to exist." "*School* fetters appeared to him of all the shackles to which human beings were subjected by the harsh customs of society, the heaviest and most intolerable." During winter vacation, when only he and Osric, a student from the West Indies, remained at school, Paul decided to build a hut ouside the school yard. Ideally, Paul told Osric, he would like to build his hut on a deserted island. Having lived on a real, not a dream, island, Osric asked Paul practical questions. Where, he wondered, would Paul obtain tools with which to build his hut? When Paul answered that he would get them from a shipwreck, Osric asked if he could swim. The difference between an idea and practical living was not simply great but irritating, and Paul replied, "No, I protest, I never thought of that. But you interrupt too much."

As the road to vice in Lady Fairfame's allegorical garden was seductive from a distance, so in the abstract an unshackled educational progress outside convention or school was appealing. However, like Master Headstrong, who found himself in the realms of Disappointment after leaving Reason behind, the child who threw off school fetters forsook reason and was doomed to fall, not necessarily into disappointment but perhaps even into destruction. As the voice of reason, Osric questioned Paul carefully about his wish to live on an island. When Paul said he would plant potatoes for food, Osric asked where he would obtain the cuttings for the plants. If he could not find them, Paul answered, he would eat native plants. How, Osric inquired, would he know which ones were safe to eat? Paul replied that he would study botany. Like the elderly female Headstrong left behind, Osric's questions were "staid," and Paul rushed ahead and built a hut, albeit in a nearby haulm field and not on a deserted island. With a rude chimney and simple opening for a window, the hut was constructed primarily from bushes and tree limbs. Inside Paul parched peas and roasted potatoes and was not remarkably uncomfortable until the evening when his schoolmates returned from vacation. Mr. Osgood met them in a coach, and as they returned to the village one of the students noticed "the uncommonly vivid effect of the setting sun upon the western sky." "Vivid indeed!" Mr. Osgood remarked, "the splendour appears more than natural!" Unfortunately Paul had set fire to his hut while roasting potatoes, and as the coach came around a corner in the road, its occupants saw that "the school-house, the village spire, and the lofty poplars, all stood in seeming darkness, as contrasted with the strong red light of the sky behind them." Because there had been a long drought, the hut, the stubble in the fields, and hedge trees "burnt with a fury inconceivable." Only a shift in the wind and the road that formed an avenue between the fields and the school saved the academy. Along with the hut, Paul's unconventional educational ideas disappeared, and he "was never henceforth troubled with longings for a desert island, or a lonely hermitage; nor ever again thought of assuming the habits and character of Robinson Crusoe."[16]

In *The Way to be Happy* (1819), a wrinkled old woman interrupted a group of boys playing. Some of the boys were so frightened that they ran away while others ridiculed her and called her a witch. Henry, the oldest boy, however, respected her because he knew she was the fairy Instruction. The youngest boy, little George, put his hand into Henry's for protection. Instruction invited the boys to visit her castle, "where she promised to make them as happy as the day was long." The path to the castle was "very much beset with briars"; eventually, though, the boys arrived, and Instruction opened the door, admitting them to a large hall where they "sat down to a pretty collation of plumb-cakes, biscuits, and sweetmeats, which were brought in by four beautiful damsels, called Innocence, Health, Mirth, and Good Humour." The hall itself was supported by five pillars, in the niches of which stood statues of Truth, Modesty, Natural Affection, Good-Temper, and Diligence. Instruction touched the statues with her wand, and they stepped down from their pedestals and gave George presents. Truth, for example, gave him a catechism bound in silver, a pocket Bible with ruby clasps, and a looking glass which revealed a person's true character, Truth said, if he departed "from mine into the paths of Falsehood." Diligence attached wings to George's shoulders, remarking they "will be of great service to you by and by; but they will droop whenever the old witch Laziness comes near." To protect him against Laziness, who would turn him into a dormouse, she also gave George a golden spur, telling him that if he stuck it into his side when Laziness approached his wings would "immediately resume their vigour." In early children's books Instruction possessed miraculous transforming powers. The journey to her castle which led to sweet rewards was difficult, and many children, books taught, fled from or ridiculed her. If a child, however, accompanied Instruction and made use of the gifts offered in her castle, he would not simply learn the way to be happy but would be happy and successful. "Modern education," contrary to Burges's contention, did not so much banish Christian from the nursery as convert "the wilderness of this world" into "that LITTLE WORLD, a SCHOOL" and redirect the allegorical progress to include this life as well as the next.[17]

Notes

1. Mary A. Burges (1800, p. viii). For John Locke's influence on early children's books, see Pickering (1981). For the conservative reaction in Britain to the French Revolution see Pickering (1976) and Sharrock (1966).

2. Axtell (1968, pp. 255–56). A Friend (1793, pp. xi–xii). *The History of Little King Pippin* (Glasgow: J. Lumsden & Son, 1814). The publication dates in parentheses in this paper refer to the editions I consulted. In many cases earlier editions exist. For first publication dates, consult the standard bibliographies: Marjorie Moon, *John Harris's Books for Youth, 1801–1843;* Sydney Roscoe, *John Newbery and His Successors, 1740–1814;* Sydney Roscoe and R. A. Brimmell, *James Lumsden & Son of Glasgow;* and D'Alté A. Welch, *A Bibliography of American Children's Books Printed Prior to 1821.*

3. *Vice in its Proper Shape* (Worcester, Mass.: Isaiah Thomas, 1789), pp. 13–14, 23–27, 35–36, 39. Axtell (1968, p. 114).

4. *The Adventures of Master Headstrong, and Miss Patient in Their Journey towards the Land of Happiness* (London: J. Harris, c. 1802), pp. 6, 18–20, 25, 35, 87.

5. *The History of Master Jackey and Miss Harriot* (Worcester, Mass.: Isaiah Thomas, 1787), pp. 5, 10, 14–18, 20–23.

6. Don Stephano Bunyano, *The Prettiest Book* (London: J. Coote, 1770), pp. 5–10, 15, 17–18, 20, 23–27, 31–33, 43, 52, 60–68.

7. Sandham (1818, p. vi). Fenn (1783, 1: ix). Fielding (1749). Johnson (1770). O. M. (1817).

8. Sharrock (1966, p. 221). Fenn (1782, pp. 38–39; 1783, 1: 50). Kilner (1783, 1: 8).

9. More (1799, 1: 12). Fenn (1783, 2: 76–77).

10. *Tales of the Academy* (London: Cowie, 1820), 1: 9, 13–18, 65.

11. *The History of Jacky Idle and Dickey Diligent* (Philadelphia: Adams, 1806), pp. 8–11, 23, 26, 28–30, 44, 49, 54.

12. Maria Edgeworth, *The Parent's Assistant; or Stories for Children* (London: J. Johnson, 1800), 3: 4–6, 30, 41–43.

13. *The Mother's Gift: or, a Present for all Little Children* (Worcester, Mass.: Isaiah Thomas, 1787), 2: 48, 66–67.

14. G. Walker, *The Adventures of Timothy Thoughtless: or, the Misfortunes of a Little Boy who ran away from Boarding-School* (London: G. Walker, 1813), pp. 5–6, 9, 16–17, 22–24, 36–38, 47–49.

15. The character has many ancestors, including, for example, the wise fool.

16. *Tales of the Academy*, 1: 137-43, 146, 152, 198–201.

17. *The Way to be Happy* (Glasgow: J. Lumsden & Son, 1819), pp. 35-40. Sharrock (1966, p. 147). Fenn (1783, p. ix).

References

Axtell, James L., ed. *The Educational Writings of John Locke*. Cambridge: Cambridge University Press, 1968.

Burges, Mary A. *The Progress of the Pilgrim Good-Intent, in Jacobinical Times*. London: John Hatchard, 1800.

Campe, Joachim. *The New Robinson Crusoe*. Boston: Thomas & Andrews, 1790.

Fenn, Ellenor. *School Occurrences: Supposed to have arisen among a set of Young Ladies under the Tuition of Mrs. Teachwell*. London: John Marshall, 1782.

———. *School Dialogues for Boys*. London: John Marshall, 1783.

Fielding, Sarah. *The Governess*. London: A. Millar, 1749.

A Friend, *The History of Tommy Playlove and Jacky Lovebook*. London: E. Newbery, 1793.

Johnson, Richard. *The Little Female Orators*. London: T. Carnan, 1770.

———. *Juvenile Rambles*. London: E. Newbery, c. 1793.

Kilner, Dorothy. *The Rotchfords; or, the Friendly Counsellor*. London: John Marshall, 1783.

———. *The History of a Great Many Boys and Girls*. Boston: Samuel Hall, 1794.

———. *Anecdotes of a Boarding-School*. London: John Marshall, 1795.

M., O. *The Village School*. Wellington, Salop: F. Houlston & Son, 1817.

More, Hannah. *Strictures on the Modern System of Female Education*. Vol. 1. London: T. Cadell, Jr., 1799.

Pickering, Samuel, Jr. *The Moral Tradition in English Fiction, 1785-1850*. Hanover, N.H.: University Press of New England, 1976.

———. *John Locke and Children's Books in Eighteenth-Century England*. Knoxville: University of Tennessee Press, 1981.

Pilkington, Mrs. *The Disgraceful Effects of Falsehood, and the Fruits of Early Indulgence*. London: J. Harris, 1807.

Rousseau, Jean-Jacques. *Emilius and Sophia: Or, a New System of Education*. London: R. Griffiths, 1762.

Sandham, Elizabeth. *The School-Fellows: A Moral Tale*. London: J. Souter, 1818.

Sharrock, Roger, ed. *John Bunyan: Grace Abounding to the Chief of Sinners and The Pilgrim's Progress*. London: Oxford University Press, 1966.

Taylor, Mrs., and Taylor, Jane. *A Correspondence between a Mother and Her Daughter at School*. London: Taylor & Hessey, 1817.

Wakefield, Priscilla. *Reflections on the Present Condition of the Female Sex.* London: J. Johnson, 1798.

West, Jane. *Letters to a Young Lady.* London: Longman, Hurst, 1806.

Wollstonecraft, Mary. *A Vindication of the Rights of Woman.* London: J. Johnson, 1792.

Wordsworth, William. *The Prelude, 1805.* Edited by Ernest de Selincourt. Corrected by Stephen Gill. London: Oxford University Press, 1970.

5   Don't Bet on the Prince: Feminist Fairy Tales and the Feminist Critique in America

Jack Zipes

For centuries now theologians, educators, literary critics, psychologists, and librarians have debated the pros and cons of reading fairy tales to children, exposing children to the cruelty, violence, and superstition of make-believe worlds. This debate began the moment the tales were written with children in mind—children as targets. From the eighteenth century to the present, serious talk has centered on the moral aspect and the related psychological effect of the *literary* tales. Yet the pedantic posture of moralism has always been suspect, for its rigidity has prevented us from focusing on the real problem, if there is such a thing as the "real problem" *with* fairy tales. Instead of examining social relations and psychological behavior first, the very stuff which constitutes the essence of the tales, *both* the proponents and opponents of fairy tales have based and continue to base their criticism on the harsh scenes and sexual connotations of the tales, supposedly suitable or unsuitable for children. Take your pick: "Away with smut and violence!" vs. "Let our children open their eyes to sex and resolve their oedipal problems!" The code words of the debate change, but there is, in fact, a "real problem" which remains: the moral attack against fairy tales (censorship) and the rational defense of the tales (tolerance) emanate from a *mutual repression* of what is actually happening in society.

Recent feminist criticism and feminist fairy tales in America have sought to confront the "real problem" that lies *beyond* and *around* fairy tales. At the very least, feminists endeavor to alter our gaze and challenge our perspective with regard to literature and society. And they accomplish this change by forcing us to look at and take our everyday occurrences more seriously than we tend to do. And every day, somewhere in America, we can read a newspaper article like this:

> Madison, Wis.—In addition to their studies, women returning to the University of Wisconsin-Madison campus are being urged to worry about something else this fall: their personal safety.
>
> The university is telling women that they should avoid walking alone on campus after dark, stay in well-lighted, well-travelled areas, stay alert, walk assertively, trust their instincts and suspicions and find other people to walk with.
>
> Women are also being cautioned against allowing someone they have just met in a bar to walk them home.
>
> Karen Hanson, a UW-Madison police detective, is also urging women to acquaint themselves with night bus and women's transit services, and the location of emergency telephones, well-lighted parking lots and residence halls on campus with open, lighted lobbies. A special security map will be available at registration to inform women about these safety precautions.
>
> The official warning apparently was inspired by the murder early this summer of Donna Mraz, a UW student from Delavan, who was attacked on campus while walking home from work alone. In addition, police in Dane County reported investigating 34 sexual assaults in June and 26 in July.
>
> Hanson advocated mandatory attendance at security programs sponsored at the outset of each school year in the dormitories.[1]

A newspaper article about murder, violence, and security measures for women. Daily events in the United States. What does all this have to do with feminist fairy tales and the feminist critique? Both the report and the event seem irrelevant for the topic at hand, and yet, often the irrelevant is more revealing than what is ordinarily considered relevant for the topic of discussion. Let us, then, probe deeper into the possible connection between rape, violence, security measures, and fairy tales. Here I want to cite another "report." This time it is from Susan Brownmiller's important book, *Against Our Will: Men, Women, and Rape:*

> Rape seeps into our childhood consciousness by imperceptible degrees. Even before we learn to read we have become indoctrinated into a victim mentality. Fairy tales are full of a vague dread, a catastrophe that seems to befall only little girls. Sweet, feminine Little Red Riding Hood is off to visit her dear old grandmother in the woods. The wolf lurks in the shadows, contemplating a tender morsel. Red Riding Hood and her grandmother, we learn, are equally defenseless before the male wolf's strength and cunning. His big eyes, his big hands, his big teeth—"The

better to see you, the better to catch you, to eat you, my dear." The wolf swallows both females with no sign of a struggle. But enter the huntsman—he will right this egregious wrong. The kindly huntsman's strength and cunning are superior to the wolf's. With the twist of a knife Red Riding Hood and her grandmother are rescued from inside the wolf's stomach. "Oh, it was so dark in there," Red Riding Hood whimpers. "I will never again wander off into the forest as long as I live. . . ."

Red Riding Hood is a parable of rape. There are frightening male figures abroad in the woods—we call them wolves, among other names— and females are helpless before them. Better stick close to the patch, better not be adventurous. If you are lucky, a good *friendly* male may be able to save you from certain disaster. [1976, pp. 344–46]

To talk about fairy tales today, especially feminist fairy tales, one must, in my opinion, talk about power, violence, social conditions, child rearing, and sex roles. It is no longer possible to ignore the connection between the aesthetic components of the fairy tales, whether they be old or new, and their historical function within a socialization process which forms taste, mores, values, and habits. And, it is too simple or simplistic to maintain that children need fairy tales more than any other form of literature to work through psychic disturbances, as many pseudo-Freudians, such as Bruno Bettelheim, have done without challenging the premise of the oedipal paradigm. It is also too ethereal and idealistic to argue that the fairy tales contain archetypal patterns which point the way to happiness, as many Jungians have done, without questioning the historical validity of the archetypes.[2] What is needed is a sociopsychological theory based on the recent findings of feminist investigations and critical reinterpretations of Freud that will help us grasp how fairy tales function historically in a mediatory role within the American socialization process.

Since the late 1960s feminist criticism has been moving in this direction. Such writers as Simone de Beauvoir, Kate Millett, Doris Lessing, Adrienne Rich, Robin Morgan, Sheila Rowbotham, Betty Friedan, and Juliet Mitchell have provided the basis for a radical analysis of patriarchal practices in Western industrial societies.[3] The major critique pertains to the power relations of domination in capitalist societies and their reinforcement by a specific arrangement within child rearing and the family. Children are conditioned to assume and accept arbitrary sex roles. These socially conditioned roles prepare females to become passive, self-denying, obedient, and self-sacrificial (to name some of the negative qualities) and males to become competitive, authoritarian, adventurous, and power hungry (again, my stress is on the more "negative" qualities, which can also have a positive side). The result of the symbiotic child-rearing process in which oppressed women assume the major responsibility for the children and the household is a type of reinforcement of the capitalist socioeconomic system in which it has become second nature for men to compete against one another for material rewards in the name of progress, to dominate their own nature and the natural surroundings without regard for the consequences. Thus social relations have become so reified and instrumentalized that we are *almost* unaware of how alienated we are from one another and how close we are to self-destruction. At least this is the warning sounded by Dorothy Dinner-stein in her book *The Mermaid and the Minotaur:*

> It is senseless, I shall argue, to describe our prevailing male-female arrangements as "natural." They are of course a part of nature, but if they should contribute to the extinction of our species, that fact would be part of nature too. Our impulse to change these arrangements is as natural as they are, and more compatible with our survival on earth. To change them, however, we need to understand not only the societal mechanisms by which they are supported, but also the central psychological "adjust-ment" of which they are an expression. What makes it essential for us to understand this "adjustment" is that its existence rests on our failure to understand it: it is a massive communal self-deception, designed to allay the immediate discomfort and in the long run—a run whose end we are now approaching—suicidal. [1977, p. 9. See also Chodorow, 1978.]

Feminist literary criticism which follows this main train of thought and deals specifically with fairy tales has stressed the positive impulse of change. That is, the criticism underscores our deep desire to change the present male-female arrangements and endeavors to demonstrate that we can raise our awareness of how fairy tales function to maintain the present arrangements, how they might be rearranged or reutilized to counter the destructive tendencies of male-dominant values. To understand the vast undertaking of both feminist literary criticism and feminist fairy tales, I want to present a brief survey of the criti-cism, then discuss major features of the tales themselves, and finally draw some sociopsychological conclusions about the utopian function of the fairy tales.

I

The feminist discussion about the social and cultural effect of fairy tales began in the early 1970s. In her article " 'Some Day My Prince

Will Come': Female Acculturation Through the Fairy Tale" (1972),
Marcia Lieberman took issue with two essays in the *New York Review
of Books* by Alison Lurie, who had praised certain tales in Andrew
Lang's nineteenth-century collections as feminist. Lieberman did a
close textual study of the tales and found that they were indeed very
much sexist: most of the heroines were passive, helpless, and submissive, and in the course of each narrative they functioned largely as
prizes for a daring prince. Lieberman questioned whether the acculturation of such normative values conveyed by the tales could foster
female emancipation. Since it has never been proven that there is such
a thing as a biologically determined role for women, she argued that
fairy tales which disseminate notions of rigid roles for male and female
characters are detrimental to the autonomous development of young
people.

Most feminist critics tend to agree with Lieberman that the traditional fairy tales spread false notions about sex roles. For example,
Andrea Dworkin speaks about the nefarious effect of these tales in the
first two chapters of her book *Woman Hating:*

> The point is that we have not formed that ancient world—it has formed
> us. We ingested it as children whole, had its values and consciousness
> imprinted on our minds as cultural absolutes long before we were in fact
> men and women. We have taken the fairy tales of childhood with us into
> maturity, chewed but still lying in the stomach, as real identity. Between
> Snow-White and her heroic prince, our two great fictions, we never did
> have much of a chance. At some point the Great Divide took place: they
> (the boys) dreamed of mounting the Great Steed and buying Snow-White
> from the dwarfs: we (the girls) aspired to become that object of every
> necrophiliac's lust—the innocent, *victimized* Sleeping Beauty, beauteous
> lump of ultimate, sleeping good. Despite ourselves, sometimes knowing,
> unwilling, unable to do otherwise, we act out the roles we were taught.
> [1974, pp. 32–33]

Dworkin examines such traditional role models as the evil stepmother, the passive virgin, the active, handsome prince, and the
powerful king to show how fairy tales manipulate our notions about
sex roles. Unfortunately, her arguments are so one-sided and crass that
she fails to make careful distinctions about the different types of fairy
tales and their effect. Perhaps her remarks are valid for the general
image of women as projected by men, which is the major concern of
her book. However, her contribution to feminist criticism about the
complex reception of fairy tales remains limited because she stereotypes the fairy tales in much the same manner as she perceives the
fairy tales to be conveyors of stereotypes for children.

This limitation is also a glaring defect in Robert Moore's essay "From Rags to Witches: Stereotypes, Distortion and Antihumanism in Fairy Tales" (1975). Moore maintains that the classical fairy tales represent the cultural values and prejudices of white people from Europe. Consequently, they must be carefully scrutinized and criticized for the manner in which they spread antihumanist stereotypes. Like Dworkin, he emphasizes only the negative features of the tales: (1) Females are poor girls or beautiful princesses who will only be rewarded if they demonstrate passivity, obedience, and submissiveness. (2) Stepmothers are always evil. (3) The best woman is the housewife. (4) Beauty is the highest value for women. (5) Males should be aggressive and shrewd. (6) Money and property are the most desirable goals in life. (7) Magic and miracles are the means by which social problems are resolved. (8) Fairy tales are implicitly racist because they often equate beauty and virtue with the color white and ugliness and evil with the color black. In sum, there is very little in the classical fairy tales which Moore would consider positive and worthwhile cultivating in the interest of a humanist education for children. Fortunately, he does not argue that these tales should be eliminated. Rather, he stresses that educators and parents should pay more attention to the dark side of the tales.

Undoubtedly there is a dark side to the tales, but within the darkness there are matriarchal remnants and humanist-utopian qualities that are neglected by critics like Dworkin and Moore. One of the important tasks of feminist citicism is to discover how and why certain changes were made in the tales during the course of centuries so that women can regain a sense of their own history and possibly alter contemporary sociopolitical arrangements. This is obviously the point of Kay Stone's essay, "Things Walt Disney Never Told Us" (1975). She compares the original Grimm's fairy tales with the British and American editions as well as with the Disney versions of the twentieth century, and the results of her study reveal that the products of the modern culture industry specify that a woman can only be considered a heroine if she is patient, industrious, calm, beautiful, and passive. Or, in other words, mass-marketed fairy tales of the twentieth century have undergone a sanitization process according to the sexual preferences of males and the conservative norms of the dominant classes in America and England. Yet Stone points to another folk tradition in America and England which portrays women in folklore as aggressive, active, clever, and adventurous. Unfortunately, these tales have been suppressed in literature and the mass media. Stone interviewed forty women between the ages of seven and sixty-one in North America to discover whether they were aware of this "other tradition." The majority of the women were mainly familiar with the Disney and sanitized versions and were surprised to learn that there were tales about independent women to which they could relate in a more satisfying manner.

The historical reexamination and rediscovery of matriarchal features in folk and fairy tales constitute some of the most important work being conducted in the field.[4] For instance, Jane Yolen, a gifted fairy-tale writer in her own right, in her article "America's Cinderella" (1977), has presented a convincing demonstration of how an active and strong heroine was transformed into a docile and submissive girl.[5] She studied different European folk versions of Cinderella and established that the original heroine had never been "catatonic" but rather had always fought actively for justice and truth. It was only toward the end of the seventeenth century that Perrault began to transform the Cinderella protagonist into a passive and obedient young woman. His adaptation paved the way for the Grimms and numerous American authors who produced dainty and prudish Cinderellas en masse in the nineteenth century. The final result of this mass-market development was the Walt Disney film of 1949, which presented Cinderella in her most "perverted" form—the patient, submissive, defenseless young woman, whose happiness depends on a man who actually defines her life. It is evident that Yolen wrote her critical essay to rectify history and suggest alternatives to our common picture of Cinderella so that women could use cultural material to realize their own essence through art and literature.

The movement toward autonomy—women should govern their own destiny and write their own history—has been a dominant tendency in feminist literary criticism, and it provided the basis for the first complete study of fairy tales and everyday occurrences. *Kiss Sleeping Beauty Good-Bye: Breaking the Spell of Feminine Myths and Models,* by Madonna Kolbenschlag (1979), endeavors to grasp and overcome the negative features in the role models of Sleeping Beauty, Snow White, Cinderella, Goldilocks, and Beauty. Kolbenschlag is interested not in the literature per se but in the habitual manner in which women are forced and influenced to adapt particular roles and identities. There are two major arguments, which are developed on a sociological and philosophical level. First, she believes that most women are conditioned to internalize rigid spiritual notions about life. Many women are religious, pious, and ascetic not because they have independently chosen their own religion or spirituality but because the teachings of the church itself have conceived normative patterns for women that hinder them from realizing their own spiritual and sensual unity. Second, she maintains that the contemporary crises between men and women are symptomatic of the feminine need for ethical autonomy that is prevented by men and institutions. Thus she calls for the destruction of the traditional feminine identity in Kant's sense of a categorical imperative. What is a given for men—the capacity for self-realization which is reinforced by the socialization process and cultural education—should be a given for women as well, but for the most part they must seek, grasp, and appropriate this capacity in ways that are painful and traumatic.

The goal of Kolbenschlag's book is to provoke both men and women to think about alternatives to the commonly accepted role models. The fairy tales themselves are not responsible for the creation of these roles; rather they are the symbolical forms which reinforce self-destructive social and psychological patterns of behavior in our daily lives. This is also the major theme of Colette Dowling's 1981 best seller, *The Cinderella Complex: Women's Hidden Fear of Independence*. Again it is not the fairy tale that is responsible for the dependency of women. The fairy tale is important only insofar as it reflects how women are oppressed and *allow* themselves to be oppressed. Dowling is of the opinion that "personal psychological dependency—the strong wish to be cared for by others—is the major reason why women today are so dependent. I call this 'The Cinderella Complex'—a network of attitudes and fears which are for the most part repressed. This network compels women to remain in the background and prevents them from making full use of their intelligence and creativity. Like Cinderella women are still waiting today for something outside them to come by and change their lives" (p. 21).

On the basis of personal experiences and empirical studies Dowling demonstrates how women themselves psychologically invent various traps and tricks to play the role of Cinderella. The significance of Dowling's book lies not so much in her analysis of the social and psychological situation of the American woman, because she remains too impressionistic, but in the remarkable connections she draws between fairy-tale images and wish fulfillment, which shed light on the contemporary dilemma of many women.

It is not by coincidence that numerous feminist critics, women *and* men, feel that the fairy tales of their childhood stamp their present actions and behavior in reality. Certain fairy-tale patterns, motifs, and models which constantly arise in our life and in literature appear to have been preserved because they reinforce male hegemony in civilization. And the exploration of the mediations between society and fairy tales seems to be breaking new ground in feminist literary criticism. In their significant study *The Madwoman in the Attic*, Sandra M. Gilbert and Susan Gubar rely upon fairy-tale motifs to examine the sociopsychological situation of women writers inscribed in the dominant male discourse of the nineteenth century. In particular *Snow White* serves them as the paradigmatic dramatization of a male-manipulated conflict between two types of females, the witch and the angel, who are played off one against the other. In their view the stepmother/witch wants to kill Snow White because the witch has become an artist who also wants to lead an active life with stealth, and the submissive, innocent, and passive stepdaughter is a threat because she has not been entrapped by the masculine mirror, and she naïvely accepts the world as it is. In contrast, the stepmother, who has learned to practice the art of black magic in a world dominated by men, no longer has any chance to attain independence. This is why she is jealous of Snow White and attempts to kill her. However, *she* must die so that Snow White can continue her role.

Gilbert and Gubar outline Snow White's future and comment on the significance of her destiny:

> Surely, fairest of them all, Snow White has exchanged one glass coffin for another, delivered from the prison where the Queen put her only to be imprisoned in the looking glass from which the King's voice speaks daily. There is, after all, no female model for her in this tale except the "good" (dead) mother and her living avatar the "bad" mother. And if Snow White escaped the first glass coffin by her goodness, her passivity and docility, her only escape from her second glass coffin, the imprisoning mirror, must evidently be through "badness," through plots and stories, duplicitous schemes, wild dreams, fierce fictions, mad impersonations. The cycle of her fate seems inexorable. Renouncing "contemplative purity" she must now embark on that life of "significant action" which, for a woman, is defined as a witch's life because it is so monstrous, so unnatural. [p. 42]

Gilbert and Gubar analyze how this basic cultural pattern in *Snow White* is linked to other images of women and the portrayal of conflicts among women in the English literature of the nineteenth century. They draw parallels to other fairy tales that ostensibly had an effect on women writers, for it is not by chance that particular fairy-tale motifs continually appeared in their writings. In fact, numerous women writers up through the present have felt compelled to confront stereotypical fairy-tale roles in some form or another to try to define their own needs.

In a lecture entitled "The Beast, the Mermaid and the Happy Ending," delivered at the 1980 Modern Language Association Meeting in San Francisco, the novelist Carolyn See expanded the discussion begun by Gilbert and Gubar. She examined how often the motif of

"Beauty and the Beast" appears in contemporary literature and discussed its significance. For instance, Alix Kates Shulman's *Memoirs of an Ex-Prom Queen,* Sylvia Plath's *The Bell Jar,* and Alison Lurie's *War Between the Tates* all depict "beautiful" women who fall in love with "beastlike" men only to learn that they do not turn into princes when the women sacrifice their lives for them. The women break their relations with these men, either to take destiny in their own hands or to succumb to a bitter fate. In this way, according to See, the novels reveal the patriarchal lie of the happy ending in the classical fairy tale.

If most feminist critics argue that the traditional fairy tales are unacceptable today because of their atavistic notions of sex roles and their ideology of male domination, we must now ask what the alternatives are. How have feminist-oriented writers tried to rearrange sexual arrangements and aesthetics to suggest that we have choices as individuals with regard to the development of gender qualities and characteristics, social values, and norms?

II

In her essay "The Tale Retold: Feminist Fairy Tales" (1982), Ruth MacDonald suggests that there are three solutions to the dearth of folktales acceptable to modern feminists: "One may present the tales, unaltered, with their traditional endings, and the devil take the consequences of the possible damage to a young girl's career expectations; one may rewrite the tales, deemphasizing physical beauty and marriage, but thereby violating the objectivity of the folklore collector by imposing one's own language and bias on the narrative; or one may write new tales, using folklore motifs with less conventional endings" (p. 18).

As examples of the new tales, MacDonald discusses *The Practical Princess and Other Liberating Tales* by Jay Williams and *The Five Wives of Silverbeard* by Adela Turin, Francesca Cantarelli, and Nella Bosnia; she finds them lacking because the male characters are presented as one-dimensional and inadequate in comparison to the females. With regard to the rewritten folk tales, she examines the two collections by Ethel Johnstone Phelps, *Tatterhood and Other Tales* (1978) and *The Maid of the North: Feminist Folk Tales Around the World* (1981); here she questions the right of an editor "who is not a teller but rather a feminist and scholar" (p. 19) to make changes that comply with her bias. Finally, she praises the unaltered folktales in

Rosemary Minard's *Women Folk and Fairy Tales* (1975) because the editor refrains from tampering with them (as if they had not already been changed!). She concludes her essay by asserting that "to subvert the ending [of a tale] by altering the reward structure or to deemphasize the essential values of goodness in a fairy tale—beauty, wealth, potency against evil, or even marriage—is inherently unsatisfying. To reconstruct the fairy tale world in the image of modernity may be possible, but success at this point in history seems illusive" (p. 20).

Perhaps it may be illusive for MacDonald, but the fact of the matter is that she is barely in a position to make such judgments when she considers such a minute selection of new and retold fairy tales. Moreover, she appears to believe that there are eternal and essential values in fairy tales which are "inherent," as if the literature were organic and as if values were natural and universal. As most feminists argue, it is this notion of biologically determined traits and values with regard to sexuality and society which needs questioning, and their experimental literature of the last ten to fifteen years reveals a fascinating transformational tendency within the fairy-tale genre that is linked to key social changes.

As I have already suggested, MacDonald has failed to indicate the great breadth and quality of experimental feminist fairy tales which seek to provoke the reader to reexamine his or her notion of sexual arrangements and the power politics of those arrangements.[6] For instance, she should have at least mentioned if not discussed in more detail the following works: *The Forest Princess* (1974) and *The Return of the Forest Princess* (1975) by Harriet Herman, *The Hundredth Dove* (1977), *Dream Weaver* (1979), and *Sleeping Ugly* (1981) by Jane Yolen, *Kittatinny* (1978) by Johanna Russ, *The Skull in the Snow and Other Folk Tales* (1981) by Toni McCarty, *Free to Be . . . You and Me* (1974), edited by Marlo Thomas, *Herbert the Timid Dragon* (1980) by Mercer Mayer, and *Stories for Free Children* (1982), edited by Letty Cottin Pogrebin, all written largely for young readers, and *Transformations* (1971) by Anne Sexton, *Beginning with O* (1977) by Olga Broumas, and *Beauty* (1978) and *The Door in the Hedge* (1981) by Robin McKinley, written for adult readers. What is interesting about the experimental "tampering" with traditional fairy tales is that the authors cut across ages, social classes, race, and gender and write their tales as socially symbolic acts to pursue alternatives to the destructive and also self-destructive processes in American child rearing and socialization.

As I have already noted, there are numerous experiments with the traditional fairy-tale repertoire that could be called feminist. Here I want to focus on a few select tales to consider primarily the manner in which writers have rearranged familiar motifs and characters and reversed plot lines to provoke readers to rethink conservative views of gender and power. The aesthetics of these tales is ideological, for the structural reformation depends upon a world view that calls for a dramatic change in social practice. My discussion of feminist fairy tales will cover narratives written for young and old. Obviously, the aesthetic complexity of tales written for older readers does prevent younger readers from grasping or even following the plot. However, *all* the tales emanate from a basic impulse for change within society, and though the writers have reacted to this impulse on different levels, they share the same purpose of questioning socialization, have influenced one another to some degree, and have been stimulated by feminist criticism to rethink fairy tales as aesthetic compositions and at the same time as cultural elements that play a role in conditioning women and children. As a cultural phenomenon, the new feminist fairy tales seek to break boundaries and speak in the name of later generations which may not need a feminist literature of this kind in the future. This is the irony of feminist fairy tales: they ultimately aim at discarding the adjective *feminist* and at conceiving worlds in which the contradictions are not concerned with sexism and domination.

In the fairy tales for younger readers the most noticeable change in the narratives concerns the heroine who actively seeks to define herself, and her self-definition determines the plot. As she moves to complete this task, traditional fairy-tale topoi and motifs are transformed to indicate the necessity for gender rearrangement and the use of power for achieving equality. For instance, in *The Forest Princess* Harriet Herman reverses the Rapunzel tale by allowing a young girl to grow up alone in a forest tower. At one point during her adolescence she rescues a young prince, and they spend several months together and learn skills from each other. He is the first one to inform her that she is a girl, but the gender difference does not appear to matter. They respect each other's qualities, and she is his equal in the forest. However, the prince misses his home and persuades the princess to return to his kingdom with him. There she encounters the prince's domineering father, who separates the two and has the princess dress in courtly fashion. The princess is upset by the double standard in the kingdom, for she learns that the girls are not allowed to ride horses, read, or dress the way they desire. So she secretly teaches the girls in her company how to read and ride. On the prince's birthday she astonishes the court by presenting a grand horseback-riding display. The prince is so pleased by this present that the king offers to grant her any wish she might have. She asks that all the boys and girls be treated equally at the court. The king frowns, and the princess realizes that her wish will not be granted. So she takes a large stallion as a present and disappears into the forest.

Herman's tale is illustrated with pictures that emphasize the key scenes of self-discovery, joy, and disappointment. The initiation ritual of this tale is totally different from that in *Rapunzel*. Absent is the female witch who imprisons Rapunzel and punishes her lover. Here the princess grows up "sexless," so to speak, and she gradually discovers that there are arbitrary sexual distinctions made in society, largely by men. She is unwilling to be socialized by such a court and rebels as an example to the other children, both as characters in the narrative and as implied readers of the narrative. Herman does not belabor her point. Neither the king nor the prince is villainous. Rather, they are stuck in a tradition that they have never questioned, and the princess as outsider can more readily challenge the authoritarian structure of the court, which incidentally begins to break down and become more egalitarian in the sequel, *The Return of the Forest Princess*.

Herman's tale obviously seeks to overcome the atavistic nature of numerous sexist folktales. This is also the case in Jeanne Desy's "The Princess Who Stood on Her Own Two Feet" (in Pogrebin, 1982). She obviously had tales like *King Thrushbeard* in mind or even Shakespeare's misogynist rendition, *The Taming of the Shrew*, all of which poke fun at and humiliate arrogant women likened to witches and shrews. Yet, clearly, the definition of "shrew" has depended on masculine images of women, and Desy is most concerned with what lies underneath the definition and images. Her tale is about a tall, young princess, bright as a sunflower, who has mastered everything she has undertaken. However, she is unhappy because she cannot find somebody to love and to love her. The court wizard, a sensitive and droll figure, provides her with a miraculous talking Afghan hound as companion, but a dog is nothing but a dog, so the princess thinks. Eventually she falls in love with a prince who has come to court her and appears to be fond of her until he asks her to dance. When he notices that she is taller than he is, he abandons her in a huff and a puff. The princess is bewildered, but her dog understands the male temperament (not that he approves of it), and he constantly advises her about how she must temper her size and skills to make the prince appear greater than he is. Otherwise he will not marry her. So she becomes clumsy and inarticulate and suffers different sorts of humiliations until she is almost catatonic. Eventually, the prince even demands that she get rid of the dog, whom he sees as a threat. She refuses because the dog has become the only creature with whom she can be herself and feel free to do as she pleases. But the dog dies for her out of compassion, and the shock of his death makes her realize "how foolish we are . . . for a stupid prince I let my wise companion die" (p. 46). So she sends the prince packing, and on the night she buries her faithful companion, she meets a strange prince carrying a banner of rebirth and bearing a faint resemblance to her dog. Though this prince is several inches shorter than she, he remarks: "It is a pleasure to look up to a proud and beautiful lady" (p. 46). They disappear into the darkness while the wizard and his cat debate the merits of sacrificing or not sacrificing for love.

Instead of passively accepting her fate, this princess takes destiny in her own hands and defines herself. In many feminist tales magic enables the female figures to grasp those forces which might keep them in a submissive position. Whereas the heroes of traditional folk and fairy tales often pursue power to dominate and rule others, the heroines of the new feminist tales use power to rearrange society and to attain independence and mutual respect.

In Jay Williams's *Petronella*,[7] a young princess rebels against her parents because she is not allowed to seek adventures and combat hostile forces. Petronella leaves home without permission to demonstrate that she can conquer an evil magician, who has allegedly kidnapped the prince she wants to marry. Through her courage and cleverness she manages to outwit and overcome the remarkable magician. However, she then discovers that her "Prince Charming" is a parasite and loafer, not really worth her trouble. So she decides to return home with the magician, a much better match for her, who readily agrees to accompany her.

Though it may be argued, as MacDonald has done, that the females in Williams's tales are much more interesting than the males, Williams does not humiliate or degrade the male characters. Some are remarkably talented and capable like the magician while others are bungling power-seekers. As a male writing to question the present sexual arrangements, Williams is more concerned about generating respect for women, learning from them, and exposing male foibles. Like the feminists, his goal, too, is the rearrangement of gender and social roles so that power is used not to gain advantage but to resolve contradictions.

The question of power is of utmost concern to feminist writers. For instance, in "The Princess and the Admiral," Charlotte Pomerantz recalls an incident from the thirteenth century involving Vietnam and the Imperial Navy of Kubla Khan (in Pogrebin). In her version the ruler of Tiny Kingdom is a lean, dark-eyed princess named Mat Mat, who is looking forward to celebrating the Anniversary of One Hundred Years of Peace. However, her joy turns to sadness when she learns that Tiny Kingdom is about to be invaded by a powerful fleet of ships.

The vain Admiral of the invading forces mocks the Tiny Kingdom because it is ruled by a woman. However, Mat Mat devises a plan to trap the Admiral and his ships by planting long wooden logs during low tide in the harbor and by luring the ships during high tide so that they get stuck on the logs like fish on poles. The ships and their crews are defenseless against the tiny kingdom of fisherfolk and farmers and expect to be executed. Yet, Mat Mat and her people send the Admiral and his men back to their Emperor with provisions to keep them alive. The princess makes only one request—that the Admiral never again make unkind remarks about women and girls. Afterward she and her people can finally celebrate One Hundred Years of Peace.

In another, similar story, "Three Strong Women," a Japanese folk-tale translated by Claus Stamm (in Pogrebin), the huge wrestler Forever-Mountain, who is on his way to the imperial wrestling matches, encounters a young woman named Maru-me, who is carrying a bucket of water on her head. He decides to play a prank by tickling her under her arm and causing the bucket to fall. But as he comes up behind her and pokes her lightly in the ribs, she giggles and brings one hand down so hard that the wrestler's hand is caught. He warns her to let go, lest he hurt her. Yet she continues on her way and drags Forever-Mountain with her. To his surprise, she is much more powerful than he is, and she invites him to the top of the mountain, where she lives with her mother and grandmother, to prepare him for the imperial wrestling matches. Since Maru-me and her mother, who carries a cow to and from the pasture, are enormously strong and might hurt Forever-Mountain, he is obliged to train with the grandmother and do menial housework until he has built up his strength. After three months pass, he travels to the imperial city, where he easily defeats all his opponents simply by stamping his foot so that they fly out of the ring. The Emperor gives him the prize money and warns him never to fight in public again since he might destroy all the wrestlers. Forever-Mountain promises him that he will refrain from wrestling, for he wants to become a farmer. He rushes to the valley of the mountain where Maru-me meets him. She lifts both him and the prize money in her arms and carries him halfway up the mountain, and then he carries her the rest of the way. It is said from then on that the rumbling from the mountaintop and the small earthquakes were echoes of Forever-Mountain and the grandmother, who continued to practice wrestling from time to time.

In the fairy tales by Pomerantz and Stamm, power is used to bring about peace and understanding, not domination. Both Mat Mat and Maru-me want re-cognition; in other words, the two powerful male figures, the Admiral and Forever-Mountain, are obliged to undergo a different cognitive process based on their new experiences with women, which, it is hoped, will alter their behavior in general. Neither Mat Mat nor Maru-me seeks revenge when attacked. They are self-confident and want to develop the talents that they have without imposing their will on anyone. All this is in contrast to numerous traditional folk and fairy tales that depict males rising to power by killing, destroying, or outwitting competitors. Often the protagonist fights for a woman or defines the woman's destiny through his heroic act, which feminist writers now declare is more degrading than uplifting for women.

Perhaps one of the most hostile reactions to the manner in which women are "heroically" treated in fairy tales can be found in Johanna Russ's fantasy novel *Kittatinny*. At one point her heroine, Kit, who is lost in a forest while undergoing an initiation ritual, discovers a story entitled *Russalka or The Seacoast of Bohemia,* which is a critical adaptation of Hans Christian Andersen's *The Little Mermaid.* Whereas Andersen affirmed the tortuous self-sacrifice undergone by a mermaid, who is eventually rewarded for this by God, Russ deplores the actions of Russalka, a mer-woman, who begins to read land books and catches the human disease, "which is wanting what you can't have" (p. 46). The fact is that Russalka despised her own kind and sought escape from the sea. She falls in love with the Prince of Bohemia and bargains with the sea-witch, who refuses to help transform her into a human being. However, Russalka perseveres until the sea-witch relents and teaches her how to transform herself back and forth. Since there is only so much a sea-witch can do. Russalka's skin remains pale, her hair green, and her blood cold. She can't speak because the thin, empty air hurts her, and when she writes notes, nobody can read them because the people at the court had not learned how to read. Nevertheless, the prince falls in love with this eccentric creature (probably because she was so eccentric) and marries her. The wedding night is a disaster because he discovers how cold and slimy she feels, and she realizes how hot and rough he feels. Russalka is bored by the chattering ladies at the court, loves to eat raw fish and go about naked. The prince becomes convinced that Russalka is under a magic spell, and since he still loves her, he sends for the court wizard to try to transform her into a lovely human bride. Russalka writes notes trying to explain her situation but to no avail. Nor is the wizard successful. Russalka wants to flee, but the prince imprisons her and takes away her writing utensils. Again out of love for her he now sends for the mightiest of wizards, who accidentally changes her into a giant frog because he has no idea of what Russalka wants or needs. Russalka is stunned and horrified, but she manages to say one word—"fool," which is meant for both of them—before she lies down at the prince's feet and dies.

Russ demonstrates in a poignant manner how a man's love can kill a woman, especially when there is no basis for understanding. Of course, it is Russalka who is at fault for denying her true essence in this tale—as she is in Andersen's. But there is a difference: Andersen was petrified of women and wanted to keep them under control, and he rewarded submissive, pliant women in his tales. Russ is angry at women who sell themselves for a "romantic" vision of love. Her tale of self-betrayal and self-denial ends on a tragic note because it is intended to serve as a warning to her fictitious heroine Kit in her novel and to her readers as well. In a man's world love can be poison, and the walls of life can feel like a prison.

Though less pessimistic, Jane Yolen also explores the mermaid theme in an original and provocative manner in her book *The Hundredth Dove*. Here two tales, "The White Seal Maid" and "The Lady and the Merman," are significant. In the first story a fisherman named Merdock traps a selchie maid, a beautiful white seal, who can also become human when she discards her fur. It is the loss of this fur to Merdock, who now has power over her, that keeps her onshore. She bears him seven sons, and over the course of twenty-one years barely exchanges a word with him. Or, in other words, she lives in a catatonic state as long as he has power over her. However, in the twenty-first year, she regains her fur and returns to the sea with her seven sons and is never to be seen again. In "The Lady and the Merman," a sea captain disdains his newborn daughter because she is so plain. He names her Borne because she is such a burden, and his grim attitude causes his wife's death. His daughter tries to live down the name, but her father becomes more cruel and bitter as the years pass. In her loneliness Borne accidentally discovers a merman and falls in love with him, especially the fish half. She cannot explain her love to anyone, but her father notices that she is disturbed and advises her to be done with it whatever it is. She takes his advice and uses all her strength to summon the merman, who travels many miles from the underworld to be with her. His act of love encourages Borne to dive into the sea and join her lover. So she becomes beautiful for the first time. And for the last.

Though the ending is ambivalent here—is it suicide or union?—both of Yolen's tales depict heroines returning to the sea, where they have more freedom. In each case they escape the tyranny of a male and define themselves. It is interesting to compare Yolen's tales to those written by men, in which the mermaid generally suffers or is punished. Yolen's protagonists are stoic and courageous, and they do not desire revenge despite their suffering. The pattern of both tales is restitution or rearrangement of roles which allows the heroines to pursue love and understanding.

In most feminist tales for older readers the patterns and themes also stress liberation and transformation. But there is a more guarded position or sober attitude with regard to the possibilities for gender rearrangement. In some cases, the writers are outright pessimistic, or pessimistic in a provocative manner. For instance, Anne Sexton, one of the first writers to use fairy tales as a vehicle to comment on the plight of women in a male-dominated society, portrays fairy-tale heroines as prisoners or commodities. She adapted seventeen of the Grimms' fairy tales in verse form to demonstrate the multifarious ways in which women are circumscribed by language and custom in daily life so that the possibility for them to attain self-expression and free movement is curtailed. In general, Sexton begins each of her poems with a first-person exposition which elaborates her "transformed" position regarding the original Grimm tale. In "The Frog Prince" she comments that

> Frog has no nerves.
> Frog is as old as a cockroach.
> Frog is my father's genitals.
> Frog is a malformed doorknob.
> Frog is a soft bag of green. [pp. 93–94]

This male frog has immense power over Sexton the poetess because he wants to envelop her in his world.

> Mr. Poison
> is at my bed.
> He wants my sausage.
> He wants my bread. [p. 94]

After examining the phallic threat posed by the frog, Sexton then retells the Grimms' story line in the third person to illustrate the situation of women in general. Her bias is clear: she is constantly concerned with the manner in which women are *obliged* to internalize conventional norms and values not of their own making which prevent them from pursuing their own desires. After all, she asks,

> Why
> should a certain
> quite adorable princess

be walking in her garden
at such a time
and toss her golden ball
up like a bubble
and drop it into the well?
It was ordained.
Just as the fates deal out
the plague with a tarot card.
Just as the Supreme Being drills
holes in our skulls to let
the Boston Symphony through. [p. 95]

Sexton describes each step the princess takes as part of a destiny planned for her by others. Though she wants to rebel against this destiny, there is literally nothing she can do to save herself. The frog is indeed a type of poison which takes on various shapes.

Like a genie coming out of a samovar
a handsome prince arose in the
corner of her royal bedroom.
He had kind eyes and hands
and was a friend of sorrow.
Thus they were married.
After all he had compromised her.

He hired a night watchman
so that no one could enter the chamber
and he had the well
boarded over so that
never again would she lose her ball,
that moon, that Krishna hair,
that blind poppy, that innocent globe,
that madonna womb. [p. 99]

Each of Sexton's transformed fairy tales is a foreboding of that fate which awaits the young woman as she matures. Actually, there is no maturation but total enclosure by male and market dictates. Such pessimism is best summed up by the ending of her "Sleeping Beauty":

There was a theft.
That much I am told.
I was abandoned.
That much I know.
I was forced backward.
I was forced forward.

I was passed hand to hand like a bowl of fruit.
Each night I am nailed into place
and I forget who I am.
Daddy?
That's another kind of prison.
It's not the prince at all,
but my father
drunkenly bent over my bed
circling the abyss like a shark,
my father thick upon me
   like some sleeping jelly fish.

What voyage this, little girl?
This coming out of prison?
God help—
this life after death? [p. 112]

Unlike most feminist writers, Sexton does not pose the possibility of
sexual rearrangement, but she does nevertheless question the present
arrangement in such a radical way that the reader of her poems must
ask why sex roles must be so destructive. There is an urgency in the
rhythm and tone of Sexton's poems which gives rise to an increased
awareness about the alienation and reification of women, about the
need to transform the socialized human condition before it is too late.

One poetess who has heard Sexton's voice and definitely heeded
her warning is Olga Broumas. Perhaps because she is younger and has
benefited from the women's movement, Broumas is more optimistic
and is convinced that there are ways for women to determine their
own lives. She, too, has transformed fairy tales into verse in her book
Beginning with 0, and in two poems that use quotations from Sexton
as points of departure she suggests another style of life. For instance,
in her "Cinderella," she begins with Sexton's statement

. . . the joy that isn't shared
I heard, dies young. [p. 57]

Here Broumas depicts the successful career woman who has broken
the male royal code; after being accepted at the male court, so to
speak, she realizes how she has betrayed her sisters and resolves to
change:

. . . A woman co-opted by promises: the lure
of a job, the ruse of a choice, a woman forced
to bear witness, falsely
against my kind, as each

other sister was judged inadequate, bitchy, incompetent,
jealous, too thin, too fat. I know what I know.
What sweet bread I make
for myself in this prosperous house
is dirty, what good soup I boil turns
in my mouth to mud. Give
me my ashes. A cold stove, a cinder-block pillow, wet
canvas shoes in my sisters', my sisters' hut. [pp. 57–58]

The answer to Sexton is sisterhood. That is, Sexton talks about this in
her poetry, but she never envisages it as a real possibility. She glimpses
the possibility in such statements as "a woman / who loves a woman /
is forever young" (quoted by Broumas, 1977, p. 59). However, it is
Broumas who then develops this notion fully in *Rapunzel*. Here the
antagonism between the old witch and the young woman is transformed into a love relationship that is celebrated. Since numerous
fairy tales, as Gilbert and Gubar have suggested in *The Madwoman in
the Attic*, often pit old women against the young, Broumas goes
against the grain and depicts the tender concern and passion of two
women. Time and again she reflects in her fairy-tale poems upon the
need for sisterhood, the need to find adequate means for self-expression. In *Rumpelstiltskin* she poses the question:

How to describe
what we didn't know
exists: a mutant organ, its function to feel
intensely, to heal by immersion, a fluid
element, crucial
as amnion, sweet milk
in the suckling mouths?

Approximations,
The words we need are extinct.

Or if not extinct
badly damaged: the proud Columbia
stubbing
her bound up feet on her damned
up bed. Helpless with excrement. Daily
by accident, against
what has become our will through years
of deprivation, we spawn the fluid
that cradles us, grown
as we are, and at a loss
for words. Against all currents, upstream

we spawn
in each other's blood. [pp. 65–66]

Whereas Broumas does not envision the possibility of bringing about gender rearrangement with men, Robin McKinley portrays self-confident, courageous young women who take the initiative in a world that they help to define with men. In her adaptation of *The Beauty and the Beast*, which is entitled *Beauty* (1978), and in her transformed fairy tales in the collection *The Door in the Hedge* (1981), it is the woman who dares to oppose tyranny, to seek alternatives to oppression. For instance, in "The Princess and the Frog," a princess loses a necklace in a well, and she becomes petrified because it is the gift of a powerful prince named Aliyander, who has come from a neighboring kingdom and is terrifying everyone at her father's court by his sinister ways. Though the princess does not want to marry Aliyander, she also knows that he has the power to destroy her father and family. Thus she must recover the necklace and appease him. A polite frog helps her, and he then asks if he can live at the castle because he finds the well so boring. She hesitates because of the terrible prince at the castle but then grants the request, for she feels that the frog might be a talisman. When Aliyander encounters the frog, he resents it and thinks that the princess is trying to mock him with the ugly thing. So he throws the frog against a wall, and the frog is transformed into his older brother, Prince Lian, whom he had transformed into a frog with the use of black magic. Aliyander now desires to destroy his brother completely, but the princess, who had run to the well and fetched a jug of water, throws the water on the evil prince, who topples and falls down dead. Afterward Lian is welcomed by the king. And the princess, too, smiles upon him as he takes her hand to his lips.

Though McKinley is often naïve and too facile in the manner in which she depicts women assuming active roles, it is this very unquestioning attitude that is significant. That is, for McKinley there is no reason why women cannot live the lives they choose for themselves if they are willing to struggle and overcome obstacles that apparently hinder men, too, from realizing their identities. Thus the evil in McKinley's fairy tales represents an outside force that disturbs the relations between the sexes. Her male protagonists are as tender and considerate as the women, and they seek to unite their forces to realize their full potential to love and create. For McKinley, the re-formation of the form and contents of traditional tales leads to a utopian portrayal of heterosexual arrangements.

Almost all the fairy tales that I have discussed explore new possibilities for gender relationships. The reversal of the traditional fairy-tale patterns is more than a simple formal matter. All the tales are linked to power, violence, social conditions, child rearing, and sex roles. How we have arranged ourselves, our bodies and psyches, in society has been recorded and passed down through fairy tales for many centuries, and the contemporary feminist tales indicate that something radical is occurring in Western society to change our social and political relations. At this point, it is fruitless to ask whether the feminist fairy tales can have the impact they obviously seek because they have not been widely distributed, nor have they been in existence very long. What is more important to ask at this stage is why they have come into being and what they reveal about social and psychological conditions in America. Here I want to draw mainly on two essays, by Jessica Benjamin and by Ilene Philipson, for my concluding remarks.

III

Benjamin's starting point is a critique of Christopher Lasch's *The Culture of Narcissism,* in which Lasch asserts that the Oedipus complex is no longer the prime organizer of psychic life or the prevalent cause of psychic disturbances and points to the erosion of a significant sense of the past and all forms of patriarchal authority.[8] In contrast, Benjamin questions "whether the oedipal model, with its affirmative view of paternal authority as a *sine qua non* of autonomy, is an ideal or universal path to individuality" (pp. 198–99). In fact, she perceives the oedipal paradigm as hindering the free development of gender identity. "The oedipal father represents our peculiar form of individuality; his authority represents the only alternative to remaining undifferentiated; his freedom up till now is the only freedom. He teaches us the lesson that she who nurtures us does not free us, that he who frees us does not nurture us, but rules us. As we shall see later, this constellation is the basis for gender domination in our culture" (p. 202). For her purpose, Benjamin focuses on the dyadic experience of differentiation in the preoedipal phase of childhood and employs Heinz Kohut's work on narcissism and the restoration of the self to elaborate her critique of Lasch.

If the decisive years of developing gender identity and individuality occur in the preoedipal phase, then it is the responsiveness or nonresponsiveness of the mother that influences the child's basic drives. The attachment to the mother and a mutual recognition of needs can encourage the independent development of a child. In the ideal constellation posited by object relations theory a child can learn to differentiate between self and other and appreciate the other's independent existence as an equivalent center so long as the mother is independent and strong enough to respond to the child's needs in the preoedipal phase. It is this phase that is key to the future gender identity and autonomy of an individual. However, as Benjamin remarks, this phase is rarely completed in a successful way in American society because the father is internalized as an ideal of absolute autonomy.

> This form of false differentiation can . . . be seen as institutionalized in the Oedipus complex and perpetuated in oedipal socialization. Man/father achieves absolute autonomy because woman/mother represents dependency. Individuality, then, is constituted by what is male, by the permanent assignment of man to the role of subject, through the father's assertion and insistence on complete independence. Originally it is through this denial of subjectivity to women that men lose the mirror of their subjectivity. Recognition occurs not through the love relationship but only in the competitive struggle with other men. Man's domination of woman has found expression in the oedipal relationships in which the split between male and female is reproduced in each generation. [p. 208]

To combat false differentiation and male domination, Benjamin insists, like Dorothy Dinnerstein and Nancy Chodorow, that the rearing of children in America must change and that men must share equally in parenting. Here Benjamin qualifies her argument in a significant way:

> But this demand covers a far broader terrain than the rearing of children. It implies a challenge to the entire sexual division of labor as well as to the separation of domestic/personal and productive/public spheres in our society. And this separation has been absolutely intrinsic to the growth of capitalism. It is this separation that, on the societal level, embodies the split between activity and recognition—the former is depersonalized and the latter is privatized. To women as mothers is assigned the Promethean task of raising individuals who can harmoniously balance what society pulls asunder. The family must bear the entirety of the individual's needs for recognition, needs that our small, child-centered families tend to cultivate intensely. [pp. 211–12]

Of course, it is well known that the family has not been able to bear this burden, but not because of narcissism or lack of paternal authority. Rather, it is the bureaucratically transfomed mode of paternal control which prevents individualization. The rise of the narcissistic personality and narcissism disturbances can be interpreted as signs of revolt against the impersonalized forces of reason which continue false differentiation and a patriarchal quest for omnipotence. That is, if we regard the narcissistic phase in a more positive manner, as a period of bonding with the mother and differentiating from this bond, then the initial goals of the child are love and self-esteem, a fundamental need for the other which can engender self-definition if this need is requited. Since this narcissistic need is rarely realized or fulfilled, it remains as a "revolutionary spark," so to speak, which can explode and engender either liberation or destruction. Whereas Benjamin would agree with Lasch that our society is becoming more callous, indifferent, instrumentalized, and commodified, she disagrees with his one-sided use of the term *narcissism* to describe the pathology. The *healthy* narcissistic longing leads in our society to a questioning of the pathology, which is the obsession with control, possession, and subordination of nature maintained by a capitalist economy and ideology of competition and rational domination. In this regard the crisis of the family and authority has a healthy side to it: the challenge to the oedipal model stems from our indomitable narcissistic longings, which have given birth to experiments with long-range goals of androgyny and parenting based on mutuality, equality, and true differentiation.

Such goals are condemned by conservative forces in American society, which are currently seeking to restore the authority of the oedipal family, with a strong father in control. Ironically, by endeavoring to move backward, the social policies of conservatism are only aggravating the contradictions within the family and the public sphere and are signing the family's death warrant. Benjamin's sober analysis of authority, autonomy, and the New Narcissism points to the necessity of further loosening oedipal structures to produce instability in the private and public spheres with the goal of generating a new form of "stable" family life that depends on mutual recognition of parents and children and equal sharing in child rearing.

Her critique is developed from another stimulating perspective by Ilene Philipson, who discusses the crisis in the family and the politics of mothering in a more historical manner. Like Benjamin, she deplores the fact that women have generally been obliged to assume the major role of child rearing; she analyzes the negative aspects of this division in the family, primarily in the period following World War II, using her analysis to understand the contemporary crisis, which consists of state intervention in the family, a soaring divorce rate, wife battering, violence against children, and so forth. She argues that "the history of the post–World War II period is a history of family life in which mothers were compelled through ideological, social and economic forces to live for and through their children. Because their own needs for recognition, meaningful work, and relationship to other adults were so frequently denied, child-rearing assumed a significance in the minds and activities of women that was historically unprecedented" (p. 61). Like Alice Miller's work in Europe (1981, 1983), Philipson is concerned with the way mothers were and are forced to play the primary role in child rearing and unconsciously engender early narcissistic disturbances by using and misusing their children in a variety of ways. The failure to develop a consistent sense of self-worth in the preoedipal phase leads to narcissistic disturbances and social behavior that are exploitative and parasitic. In the present framework of child rearing, the mother's faulty empathy gives rise to a false gender differentiation that in turn leads to heterosexual antagonisms.

> There are asymmetrical ways in which men and women come to deal with a particular situation experienced in early childhood that can result from women as mothers having sole responsibility for child-rearing in isolated, unstimulating and frequently emotionally barren nuclear families. In response to the erratic or faulty maternal empathy occasioned by such socially constructed circumstances, sons are more likely to develop a need to be admired, a fear of dependence, and an exploitative stance toward relationships with women. Daughters, on the other hand, are more likely to have a profound need to identify with and/or live through other people, to have markedly deficient ego boundaries, and to be capable of feeling good about themselves (to have self-esteem) only when they are attached or "fused" with some significant other. Both of these unconsciously based situations can make heterosexual relationships very difficult. [Philipson, p. 71]

Philipson maintains that the post–World War II family depended on sending women, who were already in the work force, back home into isolated and frustrating circumstances. Despite some changes in the work force, this policy of keeping the woman at home has been maintained to the present. Thus it is no wonder that the family is being torn asunder from inside and outside. "By indirectly aiding in the production of individuals who are incapable of maintaining enduring relationships with others, the ideology and social policy that attempts to keep mothers at home through 'expert' advice or assertion, the lack of child care, and restrictive employment practices, undermines that which it explicitly tries to sustain" (p. 74).

Like Benjamin, Philipson argues for family ties based on emotional intimacy, reciprocity, and equality, a demand that is not to be understood as some kind of idealistic declaration of rights on behalf of children and women. The feminist critique of the family and child-rearing practices emanates from a careful examination of the mediations between psychic and social structures. The conclusions to be drawn from the critique lead to political struggles in both the private and the public spheres which are still being waged. Power is at stake, and the control exercised by fathers as authority figures and mothers as their surrogate legislators will not be abandoned easily, especially when social policies do not encourage and increase individual self-esteem.

The revisions, reforms, and rearrangements in family and social life proposed by feminists such as Benjamin and Philipson are rooted in the experience of the very women and men who have already explored alternative life-styles and family living as well as alternative therapeutic treatment. Such experience is also at the root of the feminist literary criticism and the feminist fairy tales that originated during the social upheavals of the late 1960s and 1970s.

If we compare the feminist literary criticism of fairy tales to the work of Benjamin, Philipson, and other psychologically oriented critics, particularly those who have been influenced by object-relations theory, it becomes apparent that the literary criticism has *not* drawn sufficiently enough upon the studies of mothering and narcissism. With the exception of the work by Gilbert and Gubar, the literary critics have not explored the subtle connections between traditional tales which reveal the *contradictions* of patriarchal societies and the oedipal model upon which numerous tales were based. Nor have the critics made much headway in examining the new feminist fairy tales as reflecting mass social changes since 1945 that have affected the psychic structure of individuals and the general sociogenetic development of American culture.

For instance, it would seem to me important to take into consideration such developments as the "Cinderella syndrome" in writing about the traditional tale and contemporary literary experiments. This syndrome was first discussed by Jean Goodwin and her colleagues in the *American Journal of Psychiatry* and concerns girls between the ages of nine and ten who are living in foster homes and have been apparently neglected and maltreated by their foster parents. They dress in tattered clothes and are disheveled when the authorities find them. However, upon investigation, the authorities often discover that the girls do this purposely to attract attention to the fact that they are in danger of being mistreated and abused by their foster mothers, who often have case histories similar to those of their foster daughters. There are numerous questions that one could pose here. For example: Are the girls rejecting the Cinderella role by using it? Is the Cinderella role the only one they can use to draw attention to their miserable plight? What is at the base of the conflict between the foster mother and the foster child that brings about a repetition? Why have psychologists called this the Cinderella syndrome? Are there contemporary fairy tales that have explored this syndrome to some degree?

Although in fact there have been endeavors, particularly by Sexton and Broumas, to explore an aspect of the Cinderella syndrome, the point that I want to stress here is that feminist literary criticism, though more oriented toward social conflicts than the general literary criticism of fairy tales, has failed to keep pace with contemporary feminist fairy tales. In this regard, the significance of the feminist fairy tales lies in their utopian function to criticize current shifts in psychic and social structures and to point the way toward new possibilities for individual development and social interaction.

If we take the feminist tales for children and adults as a whole and generalize about their aesthetic and ideological features, we can see how closely they are related to feminist demands for gender arrangement and equality in the family and at the workplace—demands central to the work of Dinnerstein, Chodorow, Benjamin, Philipson, and others. First of all, the structure of most of the feminist tales is based on the self-definition of a young woman. The female protagonist becomes aware of a task which she must complete in social interaction with others to define herself. Instead of pursuing power for the purpose of self-aggrandizement or omnipotence, the heroine rejects violence and seeks to establish her needs in harmony with the needs of others. Power will only be used in self-defense or to prevent violence. Though the heroine may be wronged, she will rarely seek revenge. Rather, the form of the fairy tale resembles the nurturance provided by a parent who does not project her or his wishes on a child but respects the need for the child to define her or his self. That is, the aesthetic form is derived from a sense of nurturing rather than competition. Thus, there is a reversal of the morphological structure of the traditional fairy tale based on power plays and the male protagonist's quest for power.

Though it is clear that the male characters in the feminist fairy tales have other interests than the heroines, they are not portrayed in a one-dimensional way. Generally, they are associated with false differentiation or with the oedipal phase that undermines healthy narcissistic longings. However, the male characters are also capable of learning and changing just as the traditional fairy-tale form itself reveals a capacity for transformation. The aesthetics of each individual tale depends on how each writer intends to explore the contradictions of gender antagonisms, which are often linked to social problems. As we have seen, the writers who address adults tend to focus more on the conflicts between men and women and stress solidarity among women as the necessary first step to overcome the instrumental rationality of a male world. Ultimately, self-trust and trust of other women are the prerequisites for the creation of a new society. Such a society has its limitations because it tends to exclude men and exalt women, especially mothers, in a false manner. However, the critique of male domination is certainly justified, as is the dose of "healthy pessimism."

The writers who address young readers are more optimistic about forming a new world with men just as long as mutual respect is achieved. It is only in a dialectical relationship with men that the heroine, often the symbol of a healthy narcissistic drive, defines herself and has an impact on society. Though some of the feminist fairy tales end in marriage, this is rarely the goal of these narratives. Feminist fairy tales experiment with the language, topoi, motifs, and characters of the traditional tales in pursuit of expression commensurate with alternative forms of child rearing that encourage individual self-worth. To change the fairy tale, for feminists, is not simply an act of self-gratification but also a political act based on their experience in self-destructive families and on their hope that future generations will not repeat the atavistic forms and ideas found in traditional tales as well as in our lives.

Notes

1. "UW Women Advised to be Wary at Night," *Milwaukee Journal*, August 1, 1982, part 1, p. 2.

2. I have endeavored to deal with the failings of both the Freudian and Jungian approaches in my book *Breaking the Magic Spell: Radical Theories of Folk and Fairy Tales* (1984). In particular, see "On the Use and Abuse of Fairy Tales with Children: Bruno Bettelheim's Moralistic Magic Wand," which is unfortunately often misconstrued as an attack on Freudianism. My point is simply that neither Freud nor Jung can be used in an uncritical manner when interpreting fairy tales.

3. I have mainly mentioned the key figures here. Since 1970 there has been a plethora of remarkable feminist studies. For a thorough account of these works, see Elizabeth Fox-Genovese, "Placing Women's History in History" (1982).

4. Most of this work is being conducted outside of America. See Heide Göttner-Abendroth, *Die Göttin und ihr Heros* (Munich: Frauen-offensive, 1980), Yvonne Verdier, *Façons de dire, façons de faire. La laveuse, la couturière, la*

cuisinière (Paris: Gallimard, 1979), and Bernadette Bricout, "L'aiguille et l'épingle. Oralité et écriture au XVIIème siècle," *Bibliothèque blue nel seicento o Della letteratura per il populo* 4 (1981): 45–58. Cf. my book *The Trials and Tribulations of Little Red Riding Hood* (1983).

5. This essay has also been reprinted in Alan Dundes's interesting casebook on Cinderella (1983).

6. Aside from the important works by Dinnerstein and Chodorow on this subject, see Keohane, Rosaldo, and Gelpi (1982), and Gamarnikow, Morgan, Purvis, and Taylorson (1983).

7. See *The Practical Princess and other Liberating Tales* (New York: Parents Magazine Press, 1978).

8. See Lasch (1979), especially the first two chapters and the last, "Paternalism Without Father."

References

Benjamin, Jessica. "The Oedipal Riddle: Authority, Autonomy, and the New Narcissism." In John P. Diggins and Mark E. Kann, eds., *The Problem of Authority in America*. Philadelphia: Temple University Press, 1981.

Broumas, Olga. *Beginning with 0*. New Haven: Yale University Press, 1977.

Brownmiller, Susan. *Against Our Will: Men, Women, and Rape*. New York: Bantam, 1976.

Chodorow, Nancy. *The Reproduction of Mothering*. Berkeley and Los Angeles: University of California Press, 1978.

Dinnerstein, Dorothy. *The Mermaid and the Minotaur: Sexual Arrangements and Human Malaise*. New York: Harper, 1977.

Dowling, Colette. *The Cinderella Complex: Women's Hidden Fear of Independence*. New York: Pocket Books, 1981.

Dundes, Alan, ed. *Cinderella: A Casebook*. New York: Wildman, 1983.

Dworkin, Andrea. *Woman Hating*. New York: Dutton, 1974.

Fox-Genovese, Elizabeth. "Placing Women's History in History." *New Left Review* 133 (May–June, 1982): 5–29.

Gamarnikow, Eva, Morgan, David, Purvis, June, and Taylorson, Daphne, eds. *Gender, Class and Work*. London: Heinemann, 1983.

Gilbert, Sandra M., and Gubar, Susan. *The Madwoman in the Attic: The Woman Writer and the Nineteenth-Century Literary Imagination*. New Haven: Yale University Press, 1979.

Goodwin, Jean, Cauthorne, Catherine G., and Rada, Richard T. "Cinderella Syndrome: Children Who Simulate Neglect." *American Journal of Psychiatry* 137 (1980): 1223–25.

Herman, Harriet. *The Forest Princess*. Berkeley, Calif.: Rainbow Press, 1974.

Keohane, Nannerl O., Rosaldo, Michelle Z., and Gelpi, Barbara C., eds. *Feminist Theory: A Critique of Ideology*. Chicago: University of Chicago Press, 1982.

Kolbenschlag, Madonna. *Kiss Sleeping Beauty Good-Bye: Breaking the Spell of Feminine Myths and Models*. Garden City, N.Y.: Doubleday, 1979.

Lasch, Christopher. *The Culture of Narcissism*. New York: Norton, 1979.

Lieberman, Marcia. "'Some Day My Prince Will Come': Female Acculturation Through the Fairy Tale." *College English* 34 (1972): 383–95.

MacDonald, Ruth. "The Tale Retold: Feminist Fairy Tales." *Children's Literature Association Quarterly* 7 (Summer 1982): 18–20.

McKinley, Robin. *Beauty*. New York: William Morrow, 1978.

———. *The Door in the Hedge*. New York: William Morrow, 1981.

Miller, Alice. *The Drama of the Gifted Child*. New York: Basic Books, 1981.

———. *Am Anfang war Erziehung*. Frankfurt a.M.: Suhrkamp, 1983.

Moore, Robert. "From Rags to Witches: Stereotypes, Distortion and Antihumanism in Fairy Tales." *Interracial Books for Children* 6 (1975): 1–3.

Philipson, Ilene. "Heterosexual Antagonisms and the Politics of Mothering." *Socialist Review* 12 (November–December 1982): 55–77.

Pogrebin, Letty Cottin, ed. *Stories for Free Children*. New York: McGraw-Hill, 1982.

Russ, Johanna. *Kittatinny: A Tale of Magic*. New York: Daughters Press, 1978.

Sexton, Anne. *Transformations*. Boston: Houghton Mifflin, 1971.

Stone, Kay. "Things Walt Disney Never Told Us." In Claire R. Farrer, ed., *Women and Folklore*. Austin: University of Texas Press, 1975.

Yolen, Jane. "America's Cinderella." *Children's Literature in Education* 8 (1977): 21–29.

———. *The Hundredth Dove*. London: Dent, 1979.

Zipes, Jack. *Breaking the Magic Spell: Radical Theories of Folk and Fairy Tales*. New York: Methuen, 1984.

———. *The Trials and Tribulations of Little Red Riding Hood*. South Hadley, Mass.: Bergin & Garvey, 1983.

6　　An End to Innocence:
　　The Transformation of
　　Childhood
　　in Twentieth-Century
　　Children's Literature

Anne Scott MacLeod

Children's books are among the most revealing of cultural artifacts. Quite aside from whatever qualities they may have as literature,
and wholly apart from whatever effect they may have on their
intended audience, books for the young, particularly books of realistic
fiction, are rich repositories of cultural information. Like all literature,
they reflect their time and place in a variety of ways, some of them
direct, some indirect; some deliberate and intentional on the part of
the author, some far less conscious. Like popular literature (which they
resemble in several ways), children's books tend to convey conventional views more often than individual idiosyncracy, thus offering
insight into the common assumptions, the accepted ideas, and the
widely shared opinions of a culture. Above all, of course, children's
literature reflects the attitudes toward children and childhood of the
society that produces it. Both on and beneath the surface of the stories
adults write for children lie general convictions and assumptions
about what childhood is and what it ought to be, its character, its
purposes, and its place in the community of adults.

For about two-thirds of the twentieth century—that is, until the
late sixties—children's realistic fiction was shaped by a vision of childhood that varied hardly at all from decade to decade. The relationship
that obtained between adult and child in children's fiction of the
thirties, for example, can be found virtually unchanged in the fiction
of twenty-five to thirty years later. There were, of course, differences
in emphasis and nuance, and a steady trend toward writing about
older rather than younger children—children of twelve to fourteen,
say, as opposed to those of eight to twelve—but on the whole, a reader
of twentieth-century children's books written before the latter sixties

is likely to be struck by the consistency rather than by the variety of the attitudes they express.

That continuity has now disappeared; contemporary juvenile literature is a very different commodity from that of even fifteen years ago. Changes that began in the latter sixties and continued through the seventies have transformed children's books in fundamental ways, altering content, style, and, above all, the image of children and childhood (and, I would add, of adults and adult society as well) as these are presented in fiction for the young. Today's stories of contemporary realism—always the most sensitive measure of cultural attitudes—tell us unmistakably that the American vision of the ends and needs of childhood has undergone a revolution.

To describe both the dimension and the direction of change requires a point of reference. One must see where this literature once stood—what it has changed from—in order to understand the character of its transformation. The attitudes toward childhood that dominated twentieth-century children's literature until recent years are well represented in the so-called family story, a form of juvenile domestic realism that came into its own in the 1930s. These tales, mildly idealized but not heavily sentimental, presented an image of children and childhood that was remarkably enduring, lasting without substantial alteration until well into the sixties. For this discussion, I have chosen as examples the work of several representative authors of this kind of fiction, writers who were active from the 1930s through the 1940s and 1950s and, in some cases, the 1960s. Such authors as Eleanor Estes, Elizabeth Enright, Ruth Sawyer, Doris Gates, and Elizabeth Coatsworth occupied the center of the children's book field for years. Their work won major awards, appeared year after year on recommended lists, stayed in print for decades. Their books were stocked by libraries, bought by parents, and, surely, read by thousands of children. If these stories did not represent the reality of childhood altogether accurately (and of course they did not), they did record the consensus of the society about how childhood should be experienced, and about the claims of children on the adult community.

Those claims were many and strong. Family—solid, stable, and secure—was the backbone of children's literature until the latter sixties. And family was both the foundation and the chief expression of adult responsibility toward children. It was through family and particularly, of course, through their parents that children drew upon the limitless funds of love and security which the literature always assumed belonged to them by birthright.

Authors of children's fiction, however, were seldom novelists interested in exploring the variety and nuances of family life. It was the concept of family, far more than its individual expression, that dominated these books. For these writers, family was the natural setting of childhood; its value lay in predictability rather than in variety. Children's books offered a stylized picture of family life—or, to be more exact, of those aspects of family life that directly involved children—which can be taken as the authors' version of both the ideal and the actual: This, they said, was how middle-class family life worked, or ought to work, and in the few instances where they admitted it did not, they made it clear that deviance from the model was a misfortune.

Elizabeth Enright was a prominent author throughout the thirties, forties, and fifties whose work represents absolutely the characteristic tone and substance of realistic children's literature of the period. Literate, middle class, genteel, and gently idealized, her stories were acknowledged standard bearers of the genre in their time. Enright's *Thimble Summer,* published in 1938 and winner of the major literary award for children's literature in that year, is a model of its kind. The story is about Garnet, a little girl of nine-and-a-half who lives on a farm with her mother, father, and two brothers. The action takes place over a single summer, but there is no plot as such. The book consists of a loosely gathered series of episodes: a drought threatening the family fortunes breaks (a piece of luck Garnet connects with finding a silver thimble on the creek bank); Garnet and another little girl are locked in the local library by mistake after closing time; the children go to a fair; the family meets and adopts, with an absolute minimum of discussion, a homeless boy of thirteen. There are no consequences to any of these events, not even the last; indeed, Eric's acceptance into the family is accomplished in a few lines of dialogue:

> "This is someone to belong to our family," Garnet said. "His name is Eric, and he appeared at midnight."
> Mrs. Linden was the mother of three children and hardly anything surprised her any more.
> "Come in," she said. "There are griddlecakes for breakfast. While you're eating them I'll find out all about you." [*Thimble,* p. 49]

Insofar as there is an overarching message in *Thimble Summer,* it is Garnet's happiness with her life and especially with her family. "I have a nice mother," Garnet reflects at one point, "I have a nice family." Eric's appearance and his narration of his homeless wanderings have no apparent function in the story except to emphasize by contrast the security of Garnet's family life: "It made her feel safe and warm to know that she belonged to them and they to her" (p. 49).

The true theme of *Thimble Summer* is simply childhood, just as it is in most such fiction. The image of children and childhood which emerges from *Thimble* can be found again in Eleanor Estes' Moffat-family series, Enright's Melendy-family books, Elizabeth Coatsworth's *Alice-All-by-Herself*, Doris Gates's *Blue Willow*, or any of dozens of other highly recommended, widely read books from the middle decades of the twentieth century. Even the episodic structure of *Thimble* is repeated in most of these books, another reflection of the authors' interest in drawing a picture of children and childhood as opposed to telling a sustained story.

At the heart of the stories was the relationship between children and adults in general, and between child and parent in particular. Children and parents existed within a system of mutual respect, love, and responsibility, which was bounded on every side by a pervasive though rarely articulated code of duty. Responsibility took its place among the unspoken dictates of duty; that parents took care of children was assumed without discussion. Caring was more overt, though not, in this era, sentimental. Parents expressed their affection for their children mostly by their acceptance of them: "Her father looked down at her: round face, clear eyes, brown pigtails—he would not have changed her for any other child in the world" (*Alice*, p. 149).

Acceptance and mutual affection, however, did not imply equality. Families in these books functioned, gently but unmistakably, within a hierarchical order. Adults managed things, solved problems, guided and taught children. They were responsible for making life work and, one way or another, they always did. While parental rule was neither authoritarian nor oppressive, it rested upon the assumption that a natural order put adults in charge of children. And though they were seldom memorable as characters, the parents in family fiction were fundamental, providing a firm and steady foundation for a world in which children could grow up in certainty.

The children's part of the family bargain was to be affectionate, responsible, and, within reasonable limits, good. And so they were. Fictional children made mistakes, but the mistakes were minor and the children were without exception amiable, generous, well-meaning youngsters who loved their families, homes, schools, and teachers. Unhappy or unlikable children were as rare as harsh or inadequate parents in the literature; family roles were as well played as they were well defined. Parents did not bully or neglect their children; children neither criticized nor resented their parents.

The fictional children who occupied the foreground of these stories were never solitary figures in a landscape but were connected to their world by a myriad of ties. As children of their parents, as brothers, sisters, or friends of other children, and as members of the community outside of the family, young protagonists were firmly located in a human surround.

Community was a strong presence whether the setting was rural, small town, or city, and a child's growing acquaintance with the community beyond home was an important part of family stories. Most of this fiction centered on children of about nine to fourteen—in other words, on children past early childhood and old enough to expand their knowledge of a larger society. The typical narrative pattern took a young protagonist from home into the community, then back to home and family to ponder the lessons learned. Such excursions were both literally and figuratively a child's quest for experience, an initiation into the possibilities of life, and an introduction to the varieties of human personality. In contrast to the essential but shadowy parents, the adults children met on these forays into the world were often vivid characters. One remembers Mrs. Oliphant, of *The Saturdays*, with her furs, necklaces, and generous wealth, far better than the Melendy children's kindly but indistinct father; the oldest inhabitant Janey Moffat befriends is a sharper portrait than Mrs. Moffat. Clearly, their difference from the familiar was part of the point.

The conclusions a child was led to draw from these encounters were benign. Stories encouraged children to look past an unfamiliar or even an unpromising surface to find value in the people they met. Courage, kindness, and enterprise, the books said, come in every kind of package; children must seek the truth about human beings before judging them. "Sometimes people are not the way they look," Mona Melendy observes after her first unaccompanied visit to the city. "It was a great surprise" (*Saturdays*, p. 21).

Children also learned to be easy with community authority, as they were with the authority of home and parents. Ten-year-old Janey Moffat's conversation with the Chief of Police dispels her fear that she might go to jail for a childish prank: "Little girl" [says the Chief], "don't you be afraid of a policeman any more or of anything. Remember this. A policeman is for your protection. He's nothing to be scared of" (*Moffats*, p. 51).

"Nothing to be scared of" was the message, spoken and unspoken, about the world, the future, and human character. Yet it must be said that all of this exploration of the world beyond family was played out within careful limits of protection for the child as protagonist and as reader. Generally speaking, the adventures were mild and realistically probable within the realm of middle-class life. Little that was really bad or deeply frightening happened; no fictional child was ever vulnerable to a dangerously warped or evil adult. Even those stories in which children brushed against some genuinely harsh reality quickly threw the screen of adult responsibility around the experience, insuring that the child was not overwhelmed by the encounter. *Roller Skates,* written in 1938 by Ruth Sawyer, is a less homebound version of the usual exploration pattern, in which ten-year-old Lucinda leaves her stodgy family for a summer in New York with two maiden aunts. Her aunts give her a pair of roller skates and, with them, more freedom than she has ever had at home. The result is a child-sized slice-of-life novel. Day by day, Lucinda skates around New York City, making friends with city people—rich and poor, old and young, immigrant and American born. Unlike most child characters of the time, Lucinda encounters two genuine tragedies in the course of her adventures, one the murder of a woman she had befriended, the other the death of a young child she had come to love. Sawyer gives the shock of one and the sadness of the other their due, but in each case, she also provides an adult interpreter, who reconciles Lucinda's grief and ensures that these episodes will not cancel out the happier memories of her city visit. While it would be unfair to say that Sawyer trivializes tragedy, it is certainly true that she minimizes the trauma and assumes that Lucinda can act upon the adult advice she receives to "forget all about it . . . make believe it never happened" (p. 135).

The conviction that children should be defended from the starker realities of adult life was integral to the view of childhood that shaped the mainstream children's literature of the time. A child's right to adult protection was axiomatic, a basic premise, always assumed, never argued. Equally fundamental was the belief that children should grow up with confidence in the world and humankind. While the stories never claimed that people were invariably kind and good, they did insist that decency, morality, and lawfulness prevailed in American society, and they left their readers with the comfortable assurance that most trouble was temporary, that most problems were soluble, and that injustice, when it occurred, would in due course be made right. In the conventions of children's literature, it was an unspoken but also an unbroken rule until very recently that a child's story, however "realistic," must end on a note of hope.

By the 1950s, the typical family story looked to a somewhat older audience, a change reflected in the central characters, who were now more likely to be thirteen to sixteen years old than preadolescent. The age change retouched the picture of family life in the literature; authors conceded that adolescents were sometimes moody, occasionally at odds with parents or brothers and sisters, subject to waves of doubt about themselves, preoccupied with their attraction for the opposite sex.

But the differences were superficial and came nowhere near undermining the reliable solidity of family structure or calling into question the love and responsibility that bound families, young and old, together. On the contrary, fiction told young readers of the 1950s that parents understood the ups and downs of adolescence and that they could be counted on for sympathy, support, and wise advice as needed. And fictional teenagers adhered to their families with grateful affection, sometimes wishing that time and change might be halted. "Oh Mother," says a fifteen-year-old boy in a Madeleine L'Engle novel, "Why do things have to change and be different. . . . I like us exactly the way we are, our family" (*Meet the Austins*, p. 40).

His mother answers by reminding him that he will soon grow up to form his own happy family, a response which strikes a characteristic note in this decade. Family stories of the 1950s, no doubt reflecting the demographic fact that the age of marriage was dropping rapidly, offered a good deal of commentary, direct and indirect, on marriage. Parents as married partners play far more visible parts in these novels than in earlier family stories; so do the engagement and marriage of an older sister. The messages about marriage are universally encouraging: weddings are romantic and glamorous; the younger children see in them a preview of their own future happiness. More important, the seasoned marriages of parents are attractive models of loving, tolerant relationships that are both deeply satisfying to the adults and firmly supportive of the children, who grow and thrive in an atmosphere of affectionate security.

In all, then, children's literature of two-thirds of this century breathed forth serenity; it conveyed a steady certainty about the reliability of love, the essential goodness of human nature, and the rational connection between cause and effect. Books for the young child projected a calm and sunny picture of childhood; those for older readers supposed a loving, acceptable family life in which the adolescent could shelter and survive the inevitable (but minor) troubles of the passage to adulthood. Though authors made some distinctions between the security of home and the universe beyond its bounds, the general level of anxiety was very moderate. On the whole, they were far more concerned that a growing child trust than fear the unknown, and fictional children, at least, did. Cherished and protected at home, the children of the stories, both younger and older, moved outward with confidence, expecting and nearly always finding order, acceptance, and decency in adult society, learning from their contact with the larger world that there was a place and a welcome for them there.

To move from the fictional image of the world I have just described into that of recent realistic novels for children is like passing through a mirror. The most characteristic qualities of the earlier literature have been not just altered but reversed. Where there was peace, there is uneasiness, hostility, and anxiety; where there was confidence, there is mistrust. The optimism in children's fiction of earlier decades has given way to doubt and, beyond doubt, to pessimism. By the seventies, the apparent purpose of children's books had shifted from protecting children from untimely knowledge of the dark side of life to acquainting them with the worst that adult society can do and be. Not the happiness of childhood but the difficulties of growing up are the subject of contemporary realism for the young.

Perhaps the most fundamental and certainly the least subtle change is in the relationships within families. The traditional hierarchy of parents and children has been dismantled, along with, emphatically, the system of mutual respect and affection that once bound fictional parent and child to each other in peace and contentment. The literature of the seventies reveals an astonishing hostility toward parents, making parental inadequacies a central theme, especially (though not exclusively) in books written for the teen market.[1] In story after story, writers like Paul Zindel, John Donovan, Isabelle Holland, Kin Platt, and others paint devastating portraits of parents. Alcoholic mothers are legion, as are fathers who abandon their families literally or figuratively: "My father pulled that old trick of saying he was going out to buy the evening paper but went to Mexico" (Zindel, *Confessions*, p. 7). If not Mexico, then California or New York or elsewhere; the divorce rate in children's books of the seventies may have even surpassed the national statistics.

Even when they stay, parents are rarely satisfactory. Fathers are preoccupied with success and moneymaking; mothers are selfish, neurotic, unloving, alcoholic, or addicted to pills. If this fiction is to be believed, the contemporary American family is a shambles. As one narrator says, characteristically if ungrammatically, "We were the all-American family because at the core, like every other typical family, there was rot" (Scoppettone, p. 10).

Family relations, particularly between the generations, have taken on a bitter flavor. "My father . . . split the scene with some broad when I was five. He has never bothered to get in touch with me." This young man has one of the many alcoholic mothers in the fiction. She is, he explains laconically, "in an Italian haven for remorseful drinkers" (Corcoran and Corcoran, pp. 2, 23). Zindel's unhappy fifteen-year-old narrator in *Confessions of a Teenage Baboon* introduces himself and his mother in the first few pages of the book: "My story has my mother in it, and she's what is known as a small-time shoplifter." She is also, he remarks, "loud and domineering." This boy was abandoned by his father at five and has since been supported by his mother, who works as a practical nurse. His affection for her is restrained, to say the least (pp. 2, 30). The optimistic proposition that children felt gratitude toward their parents, so prominent in Victorian fiction, was muted but still detectable in twentieth-century children's books through the fifties. By the 1970s, such a concept was well-nigh unthinkable.

The misfit protagonist of Barbara Wersba's *Tune for a Small Harmonica* has "successful" parents, whose lives as their daughter describes them are sterile and whose interests do not include parenting.

> [My mother's] hair had been done at George Michel's . . . her nails at Elizabeth Arden, and her figure toned up by a French masseuse. . . . Every part of her came from a different place. . . . Every day my mother and Tippy Bernhardt did the same thing. In the morning, they shopped for two hours . . . then they would have lunch in a little bistro off Fifth Avenue, where they would discuss their friends' divorces. After that each of them would depart for a session with a masseuse, hairdresser or manicurist. . . . As for my father, who worked for Standard Oil, we never saw him. He was always in conference. Until I was eight years old, I thought Conference was a place. [pp. 15–16]

Lisa, Bright and Dark is the story of a teen-age girl whose parents ignore the symptoms of the schizophrenia that finally claims their daughter. Lisa also has successful, upwardly mobile parents—"phonies," her friend and the narrator of the story calls them—the father "caught by hard cold cash," the mother a materialistic social climber. Separately or together, they pay "almost no attention to Lisa or Lisa's sister, Tracy" (Neufeld, p. 29). The last thing these parents want to hear is their daughter's cries for help as her mental confusion overtakes her.

The books rarely suggest that the hostility children feel toward their parents is an "adolescent phase" or in any sense unjust or undeserved. On the contrary, authors are usually at some pains to make it clear that parents are not only indifferent to their children, but often openly hostile and destructive. One fourteen-year-old boy (who says his mother's "hobby" is marrying) remarks, "Mother doesn't like me.

She never has" (Holland, p. 4). Another story records a blunt and brutal conversation between mother and son. Speaking of her divorce from his father, Roger's mother tells him, "I was the one that was stuck with you. . . . I had you on my hands all the time. . . . And you were quite a hateful child, Roger" (Platt, p. 48).

The young protagonists' self-doubts—which are endless—are squarely laid at parental doors: "I'm not exactly the most beautiful girl in the world. . . . Just ask my mother. 'You're not a pretty girl, Lorraine,' she has been nice enough to inform me" (Zindel, *Pigman*, p. 9). Another fifteen-year-old introduces herself as "Suzy, the Slade daughter the father chose *not* to take to New York to live with him. My mother actually gave him his choice of girls" (Kerr, *Love*, p. 8). Though the parents in such stories are clearly unhappy people whose own lives are in hopeless disarray, authors show little sympathy for them. What counts is the effect these adults have on their children, and that is disastrous.

The shortcomings of parents are seldom counterbalanced by the strengths of other adults. Grandparents sometimes take over the care of abandoned children, as in Betsy Byars's *House of Wings* and Cynthia Voight's *Homecoming*, but in both these cases the task is thrust upon the grandparent rather than voluntarily undertaken. Sometimes unrelated adults offer the support or acceptance parents fail to give, as in Barbara Wersba's *The Dream Watcher* and Isabelle Holland's *Man Without a Face*. Of the latter two, however, one is an elderly woman who has fantasized the dramatic life she describes to the lonely boy who listens to her, and the other is a homosexual ex-teacher ostracized by the community. Both die before the novels end, leaving the boys they have befriended on their own again; what solace they provide is both brief and ambiguous. The protagonist of *Confessions of a Teenage Baboon* claims to have found a substitute for his long-gone father in Lloyd DePardi, whom he knows for a few weeks at most. But Lloyd is thirty years old, a hard-drinking, self-confessed loser who has apparently had a homosexual alliance with a sixteen-year-old neighbor boy and whose attraction for other teen-agers consists in his willingness to supply them with liquor and all-night parties. Complaints from neighbors bring the police, who beat Lloyd, then offer him a choice between prosecution on morals charges or bribery payments to keep them quiet. Left alone to decide, Lloyd shoots himself, a suicide the protagonist witnesses from a hiding place. If it is hard to find reassurance here, it is harder yet to miss in this or in most of these books the insistent message that the young cannot rely on adults to solve the difficulties of life, since adults are themselves bewildered and overwhelmed by circumstance.

Kit Reed's *The Ballad of T. Rantula* is a sad, psychologically complex novel about a fourteen-year-old boy whose parents have recently separated and whose best friend commits suicide by anorexia. The story is told with unusual compassion for both parents and child as they struggle with a situation in which their separate needs, all legitimate, are in hopeless conflict. But the collapse of the traditional hierarchy of parent and child, and the cost to the child of its demise, have never been better articulated in a juvenile novel. Fred, speaking of his Harvard-professor father and his colleagues, says it all: "They have read zillions of books. . . . They have been to more lectures than the city of Boston put together, they have written enough books to stuff five dozen bookmobiles and . . . they still can't figure out the simplest little things; what's happening, how to behave. . . . I'm only the kid, Pop. How am I supposed to know?" (Reed, p. 19).

What is lost between children and parents in these books is lost again between child and society. Though most novels of contemporary realism focus narrowly on personal events and feelings, what glimpses they give of the larger society scarcely encourage trust or confidence. The corruption that Zindel glancingly describes in *Confessions* is a major theme in Robert Cormier's *The Chocolate War,* in which a lone student is victimized by a school gang with the tacit consent of a faculty member who is using the gang to further his own ambitions. Political terrorism, bureaucratic amorality, and the helplessness of the individual in contemporary society are the central themes of Cormier's other two novels. While Cormier goes a good deal further than most writers to elaborate a vision of cold despair to young readers, he is not alone in suggesting that the adult world is a dangerous, threatening place with few shelters for the innocent. Most teen novels of recent years, and many stories for younger children as well, chronicle disintegrating families and an uncaring if not a positively threatening society.

Indeed, if security was the emotional center of the literature of earlier decades, uncertainty is at the very heart of most recent children's books. Human relationships are without permanence, and often without substance. At best, society at large is drifting, unsure of its values, unanchored by any firm belief in morality or predictability. Even a proselytizing author like Madeleine L'Engle, whose novels are a vehicle for her spiritual and moral convictions about the power of love, conveys little faith in human decency outside a cultured elite, and less confidence that the chaos of modern life can be held at bay for long. So Meg Murry, in *A Wind in the Door,* reflects on recent problems in her hometown: "Suddenly the whole world was unsafe and uncertain. . . . Even their safe little village was revealing itself to be unpredictable and irrational and precarious" (p. 33). At worst, books like most of Zindel's and all of Cormier's describe a nightmare world of violence, betrayal, and irrationality which offers no place, not even home, where a child may grow up in safety.

Within this uneasy setting, the central characters of recent fiction exist in virtual isolation. Remembering the cheerful clumps of children in family literature of earlier decades, one realizes how often current protagonists lodge in the mind one by one: Adam, the doomed child of Cormier's bleak *I Am the Cheese;* Slake, living like a rat in the New York subway in Holman's *Slake's Limbo;* Flanders, in M. E. Kerr's *Is That You, Miss Blue?;* and John, the quintessence of loneliness and central character of Donovan's *Wild in the World,* who sees his family die one by one and then dies himself, alone. Or one remembers pairs of kids clinging to each other for the comfort and reassurance they cannot find in adults, as in June Jordan's *His Own Where,* Rosemary Wells's *None of the Above,* and most of Zindel's novels for teens.

A corollary to the isolation of the protagonists in these novels is their self-absorption. Forty or fifty years ago, authors implicitly identified one central task of growing up as the transcendence of egocentricity. The pattern of fiction encouraged children to become acquainted with their communities and their fellow human beings, to find their place in the society beyond home. Personal growth was measured and maturity defined by a child's growing understanding of and concern for other people.

Today's authors, by contrast, presuppose an adult society so chaotic and untrustworthy that no child could move toward it with confidence. Its rules are unclear, its authorities corrupt or ineffectual, its values bankrupt. Most of all, it is a society inhabited by people who are manifestly unhappy. By the same token, closeness with another human being is as likely to end in disillusionment as understanding; love is more often a source of pain than of joy in these books. Any encouragement to go outside of one's self is cautious at best, and most protagonists are, in fact, mainly preoccupied with self. Their problems, their emotions, their reactions and needs occupy the center of the literature, and neither challenge nor perspective is added by the authors. Judy Blume's enormously popular books, which mirror the egocentricity of childhood and adolescence without comment and certainly without criticism, are the best-known but hardly the only examples of a general abandonment by contemporary authors of the traditional adult determination to modify the self-centeredness of children. It would be hard to overstate what a breathtaking change this represents over *all* past American literature for children.

It is impossible to read very much of this fiction without raising some questions about the cumulative sense of bitterness and disillusionment that pervades it. What accounts for such a drastic revision of the traditional tenets of literature for children? What is the impulse that has toppled the age-old relation of child to adult, which assumed the superiority of adults and the need of children to learn from their elders? Authors of the seventies have opened the secrets of the adult world to children as juvenile literature has never before done. They have demolished protective walls built well over two hundred years ago to separate the child's world from that of the adult, and in doing so, have not only exposed children to aspects of adult life long considered unsuitable for them to know, but also and by the same stroke have exposed adults to the scrutiny of children who now see them portrayed in every shade and degree of failure, inadequacy, and confusion. What kind of cultural change has brought about such a development?

It is far easier to ask the questions than to answer them. Any search for the sources of cultural attitudes may encompass every influence on a society and cross the entire political and social spectrum. The enormous upheavals in American society in the sixties and seventies coincide with the advent of a "new realism" in literature for children, and there is undoubtedly some causal relationship, however complex. The social and political struggles of those years set in motion powerful forces for change in American society, changes that must have inevitably affected the tone and tenor of literature written for the young as they affected so many other traditionally accepted conventions.

The relationship between societal unrest and the mood of children's books, however, is not a simple one. The image of trust and tranquillity in children's books of the thirties, for example, contrasts sharply with the anxieties of current fiction, yet the 1930s can scarcely be called a tranquil period. In a decade darkened first by economic depression, then by world war, millions of families knew that life was hard, uncertain, sometimes terrifying. Nevertheless, the thirties produced a literature for children that promised them the shelter of adult protection, a future with hope, and the assurance that happiness was attainable—all propositions that the fiction of our own era has effectively reversed. At the very least, we must conclude that the turmoil of the past fifteen to twenty years has done more damage to traditional familial arrangements than did either depression or war in the 1930s and 1940s.

Cause and effect in cultural change are notoriously difficult to demonstrate. Confident assertions about the precise ways in which the political and social disturbances of recent years have revolutionized the concept of childhood in children's books would go well beyond both my purposes in this essay and the slender evidence available. But to read the books is surely to ponder the nature, if not the exact sources, of the changes I have described in attitudes toward children, and some observations, admittedly highly speculative, about the emotional meaning behind these attitudes are irresistible.

The chief casualty of the new realism has been the clear separation between adult and child observed in over two hundred years of writing for children. And the blurring of the distinction has taken place in both directions. The child, as recipient of knowledge hitherto withheld, is increasingly treated like an adult. At the same time, adults, with their open uncertainties, their unwillingness to carry the burden of responsibility, their preoccupation with their own satisfactions, function more like children, or at least like adolescents, than ever before in juvenile literature.

Certainly the tone of the literature is authentically adolescent. Egocentric, emotional, angrily judgmental toward adults, the stories purportedly reflect the outlook of their young protagonists. But I cannot escape the feeling that the emotion these authors put into their stories of family life is their own as much as it is that of their fictional characters. Surely it is significant that the first-person narrative, which fuses the voices of author and protagonist, is all but universal in recent teen fiction. First person was rare in earlier children's books; then adults stayed firmly in their adult place, protecting, instructing, assuming the superiority of adult knowledge and judgment, and translating that sense of superiority into an unargued acceptance of responsibility for children. Even if it is no more than a literary device, the use of the first-person voice has effectively diluted the separate adult presence one could always detect in children's books of the past.

Implicit throughout the new realism is a cumulative assertion of the failure of human relations in general and of adult-child relations in particular; the persistent mood is one of resentment and despair. As conclusions, both seem to be largely unconscious on the authors' part. Even in strongly realistic stories, today's authors generally accept, at least overtly, the convention that books for the young must conclude on a positive note. The endings of choice in recent fiction are hardly stridently optimistic, but most authors (Cormier always excepted) extend to their characters and readers assurances that their feelings are normal, that they will adjust and survive whatever crisis they are facing.

Yet the unspoken communication is the more powerful; it is hard to balance by such tardy and bland reassurance the bleakness that dominates the books. The aggrieved tone of the fiction overwhelms its stated sentiments, as the passionately one-sided portraits of parents project the dismay of an adolescent who has discovered that parents are human and flawed, and that the society at large is neither safe nor happy. One ends by believing that the authors are as angry with adults, as outraged by the failures of adult society, as any of their fictional characters. And one cannot but speculate that these authors, children as they are of the thirties and forties, are recording the dislocation of a generation brought up to expect a contentment it cannot find in the contemporary world.

In general, realistic fiction of recent years conveys an image of adults withdrawing from parenthood, retreating, in a real sense, from adulthood. The settled hierarchy of adult-child relationships is destroyed, and with it the system of responsibility and dependency that firmly separated child and adult roles. It is no longer taken for granted that adults are moral mentors to the young. Adults in fiction, and the adults who write the fiction as well, seem to have little impulse to define the moral world for children. At most, they heap their readers with information and step back from decision, and from the responsibility that decision implies. In any case, much of the fiction tends to concentrate on a kind of therapeutic "working through" of feelings rather than on moral decision; not resolution but coping is the aim. As implicitly defined, coping means minimizing pain, tolerating disappointment, accepting one's own feelings, and, above all, limiting one's emotional investments. Insofar as the books endorse any goal, it is survival, not mastery; endurance rather than triumph. Such tepid conclusions are of course offered as realistic, as sharper resolutions would not be. I do not argue the point; I would only note the abyss that lies between such a view and that which informed children's literature of the past. Into the abyss has fallen hope, conviction, moral certainty, optimism, and, possibly, courage.

Like so much else about these novels, their moral neutrality is symptomatic of a deeper shift in the adult stance toward the young. Nothing in the literature is more striking than the sense that adults have lost confidence in their ability to tell children how to live in the world. Their unwillingness to describe and prescribe "right" behavior for children, their evident dissatisfaction with their own lives, the guilt that takes the form of inviting the condemnation of adults by children—all betray how little these authors, and the adults they speak for, believe that they are in a position to tell children how things ought to be. No matter what else they know, as the protagonist of *T. Rantula* pointed out so cogently, they seem helpless before the fundamentals of living: "what to do, how to behave." They decline to decide for children what is right because they no longer believe that they themselves know. Even experience, that time-honored trump card of adults, avails them little. Adults as the fiction portrays them are lost in a world in which the rules are other than those they learned, or in which there are no rules at all.

It would be neither surprising nor unprecedented if a faltering adult confidence in contemporary society resulted in literary romanticization of the young as more sensitive and natural than adults. There is some: *Lisa, Bright and Dark* and Paul Zindel's teen novels reflect some neoromantic notions about children as better human beings than adults. But today's romanticizing, when it occurs, is a far cry from the late-nineteenth-century vision of children pure in heart and charming in manner leading adults to a more moral life. The children of contemporary fiction work no miracles on the people or the world around them—no one believes in miracles any more—and they have few of the charms of their romantic predecessors. Indeed, given their universal self-doubts, their waspish criticism of almost everyone, and their entire preoccupation with their own, usually negative, feelings, today's protagonists are often pitiable but rarely lovable and almost never admirable. Though the style of contemporary adolescent fiction still sounds faint echoes of J. D. Salinger, few of its heroes are as warmly compassionate toward a world they never made as was that early neoromantic creation, the *Catcher in the Rye*. Even after Victorian sentimentality had passed out of fashion, a modest idealization of children persisted a long time in literature for the young, but no romantic bloom seems to have survived the chill winds of recent history.

Finally, when the awful weight of negativism is measured and the failures, disappointments, and betrayals in contemporary children's books are tallied together, another observation is hard to avoid: the literature is fundamentally anti-child. Something in the eagerness of the authors to acquaint children with all the terrors of the contemporary world, in their unwillingness to offer any perspective or corrective to puerile emotions, something in the joylessness of the fiction as a whole, goes beyond the requirements of an unflinching realism designed, as its apologists claim, to prepare children for the real world. From an obscure level, and surely without conscious intention by the authors, much of current fiction communicates an adult hostility toward children and, ultimately, toward the very concept of childhood. For while childhood is in one sense a biological reality, in another it is a cultural creation. As a distinctive period of life lived under adult protection and sheltered in some degree from adult concerns, childhood exists if, and only if, adults are willing to accept the burden of responsibility such a system imposes upon them. It is too soon to know whether the adult resistance to childhood's claims which runs like a subterranean stream through recent juvenile fiction is a passing or a permanent phenomenon. What is certain, I think, is that contemporary American culture is profoundly ambivalent about children, unsure whether they are dependents, companions, or adversaries. Children's literature reveals that ambivalence, perhaps better than almost anything else.

Note

1. The concentration of harsh realism in novels of teen-agers does not account for the change in tone, though at first glance it may seem to do so. The teen novel, after all, flourished for nearly twenty years before benevolence vanished from its portrayal of family life. Moreover, by the seventies, children's books at every level reflected a less idealized view of childhood, though books for under-twelves were less overtly cynical than were those for adolescents. In any case, the significant fact is that by the seventies, the adolescent novel, with all its negativism, *was* the characteristic realistic fiction of the period; the family story for preadolescents was in decline. Clearly, what authors had to say about the American family they considered best suited to an older audience. And perhaps as clearly, authors believed that teen-age readers would find these jaundiced accounts of families and family life true to their own experience.

References

Byars, Betsy. *House of Wings.* New York: Viking, 1972.

Coatsworth, Elizabeth. *Alice-All-by-Herself.* New York: Macmillan, 1941.

Corcoran, Angier, and Corcoran, Barbara. *Ask for Love and They Give You Rice Pudding.* New York: Bantam, 1979.

Cormier, Robert. *The Chocolate War.* New York: Pantheon, 1974.

———. *I Am the Cheese.* New York: Pantheon, 1977.

Donovan, John. *Wild in the World.* New York: Harper & Row, 1971.

Enright, Elizabeth. *Thimble Summer.* New York: Holt, Rinehart & Winston, 1938.

———. *The Saturdays.* New York: Holt, Rinehart & Winston, 1941.

Estes, Eleanor. *The Moffats.* New York: Harcourt, Brace & World, 1941.

Holland, Isabelle. *The Man Without a Face.* New York: Lippincott, 1972.

Holman, Felice. *Slake's Limbo.* New York: Scribner's, 1974.

Kerr, M. E. *Is That You, Miss Blue?* New York: Harper & Row, 1975.

———. *Love Is a Missing Person.* New York: Harper & Row, 1975.

L'Engle, Madeleine. *Meet the Austins.* New York: Vanguard, 1960.

———. *A Wind in the Door.* New York: Farrar, Straus & Giroux, 1972.

Neufeld, John. *Lisa, Bright and Dark.* New York: Phillips, 1969.

Platt, Kin. *The Boy Who Could Make Himself Disappear.* New York: Chilton, 1968.

Reed, Kit. *The Ballad of T. Rantula*. Boston: Little, Brown, 1979.

Sawyer, Ruth. *Roller Skates*. New York: Viking, 1936.

Scoppettone, Sandra. *The Late, Great Me*. New York: Putnam's, 1976.

Voight, Cynthia. *Homecoming*. New York: Atheneum, 1981.

Wells, Rosemary. *None of the Above*. New York: Dial, 1974.

Wersba, Barbara. *The Dream Watcher*. New York: Atheneum, 1969.

——. *Tunes for a Small Harmonica*. New York: Harper & Row, 1976.

Zindel, Paul. *Pigman*. New York: Harper & Row, 1968.

——. *Confessions of a Teen-age Baboon*. New York: Harper & Row, 1977.

7 The Culture of My Childhood

Roger Sale

I went to graduate school in English at Cornell, in the town where I grew up and where my father was a famous and popular English teacher. My status as a faculty child gave me free tuition, which is why I was there; other aspects of being in a school and a department where my father taught made me nervous, not least among these being the frequent suggestion made by other graduate students that I had an unfair advantage over them because I was raised in a house full of books. I resented this, because it gave me no credit, and because I was beginning to overcome an idolizing fear of my father and to see that, as a father, he had not been a good bargain. Furthermore, in my childhood, books meant little to me. They furnished rooms, and they invariably baffled me when I tried to read one of them. Indeed, when at age twelve I finally did read a book that mattered to me, my childhood was thereby beginning to end.

William Sale, who dominated a household in which he was not actually present much of the time, was a great knower, but not really a cultured man. He had little use for anything not cognitive—for music, dance, the visual arts, manners, charm, gossip in the good sense, enthusiasm, partisanship, passions, or for odd and curious instances except as they might be found in language. Whatever advantages he gave his sons had to do with what he knew and with the insistent ironic control he exerted over other people by means of knowledge. "Know ye not mee," says Satan to some lesser angels outside Eden, "Not to know mee argues yourselves unknown." Father would ask after a person, place, date, or title. One or the other of us would draw a blank. Father's voice, triumphant, ironic, amused, would fill the room. "Know ye not Athos (or Sofia, or James G. Blaine)? Not to know that is to argue yourself unknown." I charted

118

courses by the fear of arguing myself unknown. I learned a lot, to be sure, so that whenever I tried to explain the matter to graduate-school friends, their reply, itself triumphant, ironic, and amused, would be "See!" For them the numb fear, the endless nagging guilt, the awareness that someone else nearby knew more and decided what was worth knowing, were unimportant, the necessary bruises that came with the territory. They could see only the green grass on my side of the fence. Imagining riches over there, they had little interest in imagining the position of one who knew these riches only as a game. In that game I always had enough coins to play, and therefore I could not beg off, but never enough to play well, or to win, or to see that there were any riches.

As I essay the culture of my childhood, I need to note that I was born in 1932, in a suburban enclave of a small university city in upstate New York; I want to mark the obvious appurtenances and signs of a culture—such as pictures, books, radio programs, movies, ritual, and improvised games—and the family, neighborhood, and school life surrounding me. But I want to present these from the inside out, not as an analyst or a sociologist might reconstruct them, but as I remember them, as I felt them then. I want something that can set me at least a little apart from Bill and Kirk, my older and younger brothers, who shared so much of them with me. Something that can show what, as I emerged from childhood, I took life to be, something that would shape what my actual life would become. I exclude my earliest years because I have little memory of anything before age four, and because the pursuit of those years might lead to findings about my person or my psychology, but little about my culture. Not that I can draw a clear line between person and culture, or between autobiography and essay; nor that I can or wish to define "culture." With my earliest years, however, I would be working almost entirely with what others have told me, whereas from about age four on I have enough clear memories to claim the experiences as my own.

Start with tasks, commands given by some adult that had to be repeatedly obeyed. Frost says that fact is the sweetest dream that labor knows, but that was seldom apparent to me as a child. In 1939, when I was seven, the family moved to 309 The Parkway, a new house with a three-quarter-acre lot. For a time Bill and I were given a dime for every bushel of stones and weeds we collected. For the next ten years we got a dime each for mowing half of the immense lawn. There were other chores—shoveling snow, taking out the garbage, hauling prunings, turning over soil, and rolling the lawn in the early spring—but mowing is the task I most remember, and, remembering it, I gave up quickly on my own efforts to engage my children in mowing the much smaller lawn they grew up with. I was aware that the tasks were unskilled, and that any labor that might yield the sweet dream of fact, like planting a garden, or working with wood or metal, or repairing anything, was presumed to be beyond me. For as long as I can remember, this presumption of my clumsiness is there, though I was not told that one reason for this clumsiness is that I am almost blind in one eye and have poor depth perception. This might have limited my skill at tasks that require really good eye-hand coordination, but it hardly explains why I could not tie my shoes for years, or button a button fly, or why I was never allowed near a package of seeds, or a hammer and nails. Rather, I think, Father needed certain handles to understand his children, and one of his handles for me was that I was uncoordinated. My sense that work was onerous arises, thus, from the fact that the work I was given to do was onerous.

Spring was the worst time with the lawn, especially when Bill went away to school for a year and often found ways of begging off after that. Spring is brief in upstate New York, and the lawn would go almost overnight from barren to teeming with dandelions and grass. If, as usually happened, it rained a lot, the grass got massively high before it could be cut at all. I would do a patch, see all too clearly how much was left, quit, and secretly hope for more rain so the remainder could be postponed, ignoring the certainty that more rain meant a still harder job and a sooner remowing. It helped little when I got other mowing jobs, for thirty-five cents an hour or fifty cents a job, on easier and smaller lawns. I nurtured my resentment of the low pay, of Bill's greater strength and his being able to say his asthma prevented him from mowing, and of my never being given more skilled tasks.

Grade-school math was almost as bad, though here I knew there was nothing unfair about it. From grades three through eight—three-digit multiplication, long division, fractions, decimals, percents, word problems—it always seems to be early afternoon in winter, the over-head lights are on, and we do problems endlessly. Parodies, they might seem, of my household chores: if Mike gets 12¢ / bushel for digging potatoes, and if he can dig three pecks an hour, how much can he make in three days, digging six hours a day? What percent of what Mike makes can Pete make if he digs $1^1/_4$ pecks an hour? I never saw any beauty in a mowed lawn, and was unimpressed by results in arithmetic, so I seldom got more than two or three consecutive problems right. I was also aware that some others, mostly girls, did better because they made neat, lightly drawn numbers and few erasure marks. If it was worse for me than for others, that was probably because I understood none of it; it was much later when I saw why $1/2 \times 1/2 = 1/4$, or why long division is done the way it is.

Here culture is strictly command felt as weight, numbness, and dread. I mention these activities not to suggest that my lot was particularly hard, but to show their contribution to two related feelings that were usually with me: there was much others could do that I could not, and if life could be intelligible only in compartmented areas, then it was into those areas that I would pour myself. The most important of these were the games, and while the role I played in these games was not the happiest, it was much preferable to that of mower or arithmetician. Father had no other or better way of dealing with his children than these competitions. When I was, say, eight, Bill was eleven and Kirk three; when I was eleven Kirk was still only six. So for most of my childhood I was destined to lose to Father or to Bill. We had many board games, *Monopoly* and *Boake Carter: Star Reporter* being the best; card games, *Authors, Flinch, Pit, Rook,* and later on there was bridge, which Mother joined in on after dinner. We had lots of chess and spurts of Chinese checkers. There was constant quizzing at meals. Books of questions about history and geography, puzzles ranging from scrambled letters—"cashnip" can be made into what vegetable?—to "Three men went into a hotel and paid $30 for a room" and "There were three Pilgrims and three Indians by a river." Not to know that Baltimore is larger than Boston, or how a man can be his own grandfather, was to argue oneself unknown. Father did not get into games he could not win, and Bill was always a step or two ahead of me, so I played only to stay close, to remember next time, or to argue myself slightly less unknown. This I could do and enjoy doing, especially compared to the numbing chores, so that while being competitive seemed natural, I did not mind (and never have much minded) losing. Something like a real hunger to know came later for me, and probably always has been tinged with the desire to catch up or show off. As a child others were always choosing the games and the desirable knowledge; what I learned on my own, like the names of cities in the USSR that I got from war maps, or hordes of baseball statistics, or the characteristic postage stamps of different countries, were ceded to me, and no one would compete.

There were consequences of having a cognitive and competitive heart to my culture, some of which might surprise others raised differently. For instance, I tended to ignore my younger brother, since he was too young to take part and no fun to defeat when he got to be old enough. Another kind of play, more mindless but also more inventive and free, in which age differences matter less, was almost unknown to me; the only thing I can remember doing with Kirk in his earlier years

was making dams of mud and sticks along the curb in late winter
when snow was melting. Or, to take another instance, the quality of
sounds of laughter. Father's laughter was knowing and ironic, usually
tinged with derision; as one might imagine, giggling in our house was
a sign that one was out of control and was reproved. The only laughter
I heard that was not associated with the triumph of knowing, or
getting a joke, or ridicule came from my mother when she was with
adults other than Father. I will speak at greater length of my mother
later; in this context I need only note that though she would play card
games after supper, to make a fourth or to keep the family together,
most competing was alien to her. We discovered once that she did not
know if Iowa is east or west of the Mississippi and did not feel herself
argued unknown by her ignorance. It was hard to know how to deal
with that, and so I came to assume there was a connection between
uncompetitiveness and women, which did nothing to help my spas-
modic attempts to understand them.

In sports I suffered from being a year younger than everyone in my
class and from my defective depth perception. I did have good sprint
speed, though, and one might have thought that mattered, and it
did, but in odd ways. It mattered in fourth-grade football, when I was
known as half the team because I scored 48 points in a 96-0 win over
the third grade. But that was strangely forgotten in our first choose-up
game the following fall; I was picked fourth or fifth or later and given
appropriately smaller roles in which speed mattered little. I won sprint
races in city-wide competitions as a Cub Scout, but there I was running against boys my age, and that counted very little with the boys in
my class in school. We had one year where we played a lot of soccer,
but for some reason I was goalie most of the time, a job which
demands no speed but does ask for quickness and good vision, which I
didn't have. But there was no question of not playing, or not wanting
to play, and it was hardly news that powers I had seemed less important than those I lacked.

There were deeper consequences. In my father's pantheon there
was nothing, at least theoretically, not worth knowing, though there
was much he was not interested in. Anyone could gain his admiration
by working hard at learning something, or how to do something. My
brother Bill was often commended for taking long hours to work at a
piece on the piano, staring at a chess problem, fixing a bicycle, or
playing with his chemistry or erector set. When Father took up gar-
dening or golf, he would get a stack of books on the subject and slowly
make his way through it. When I was about ten, he spent an entire
summer on the history of the Southern Pacific railroad as a spinoff
from teaching Frank Norris's *The Octopus*.

I knew all this, but could not emulate these models. One might well ask why, if I wanted to beat Father or Bill at chess, I did not work harder at it; if I had become a really good player, nothing would have pleased Father more. But I played, not in order to lose but assuming I would, and this inhibited my sense of my ability, or possibilities. I would replay famous games out of books, but to get the drama, the thrilling sacrifice, the wonderful rescue, and never asked hard enough how these wonderful things came about. Often, in a game, I would play ten or fifteen moves well enough because I had learned them by rote; often I then might gain an advantage in the middle game that, it seems invariably, I would squander in one or two careless moves that showed my lack of understanding of my advantage. After the game was over, Father or Bill might then want to go back and study the crucial point to see what I should have done, but I would just want to play another game. Chess continued to fascinate me, as bridge did later, but in both games I soon reach my limits. In a quick-action game like poker, I am very good.

Thus, when I hear or read of others who suffered through childhood miseries alone, withdrawn, reading, rich in fantasy, taking long walks, making things with wood, getting good with a musical instrument, I always feel a twinge of envy. There, I feel, is someone who really felt life, who plumbed some of its depths in unhappiness greater than any I knew. There, I feel, is someone who carved an individual way, and earned a real measure of independence and identity. I learned to be a decent companion for myself, but was too socialized, too committed to the game, to be able to stick with anything designed to be done alone. When by myself I had a pathetically short attention span, and even now, when I look forward to spending a day with a task, I find I read, or write, or garden, in spurts, the day breaking up into chunks of this or that. I had piano lessons for years, but never was more than a beginner. I learned to read quickly, but when I was quite young my parents started complaining that I seldom finished a book. When, in the fifth and sixth grades, many of us in school started bird watching, I entered as if into a competition, but soon discovered I seldom spotted a bird smaller than a robin, and so had to fake it, and often in the field would forget what I had learned in a book. Bird watching is something one learns to do, and it takes time and patience, but I cut myself off from it by assuming too quickly that I would never learn.

But I was not depressed, and did not suffer from a desperately low self-esteem; those, one might say, were for people more real, more deeply etched by life, than I was. I got used to and accepted my role as the clumsy one, as the loser. Thus, when I tell someone now that

Father often said you could tell what we had for dinner by looking under my place, or, watching me eat, would turn to Bill and say *"That's* not a horse," the response is pity or outrage. But I felt little of that, since such remarks seemed to come with the territory of being me. As long as I played my role, I could be part of the group, tag along, play along, and be surprisingly content. If I felt really miserable, I might go off, and even resolve never to speak again. Being called to dinner, I might then be silent for a few minutes, but if I was asked to name the states whose capitals are also their largest cities, I was hooked, talking: Boston, Atlanta, Little Rock, and so on.

In all this, my strongest ally and best companion was my mother. While growing up, if that fact needed remarking on, it was said that we both liked to get up early, or did chores cheerfully. In fact, in that family we both had roles, and we were both second-class citizens. Father would never have turned to her to say, about my eating, *"That's* not a horse," because she, we all knew, did not play such games and did not think them fun. Yet she explicitly accepted all my father's values, or, more precisely, though she was a very different person, never went against their dictates and would reprimand any rebellion against them. Hers were the lessons I could not learn since they spelled a kind of victory I would not understand and a kind of defeat I had to fear. Had I really followed her, or tried to emulate her, she herself would have been alarmed.

Mother was kind, patient, and quickly forgiving. She was for uncompetitive fun and easy laughter. Though she seldom spoke about herself, she was constantly remembering what others did, loved to reminisce, and effectively gave us a gallery of people we knew little or not at all but about whom we knew stories or odd traits. Mother was music, from Bach to the most recent popular song. She was for conversation and for any kind of gathering where people had fun, weren't solemn, and weren't competitive or mean. She insisted on not taking herself seriously. She placed against the kitchen wall a small placard that began "Why were the saints saints?" It continued with phrases like "They were patient when they wished to be impatient" and "They went on when they wanted to stop" and ended "It is quite simple and always will be." By such a reckoning, she was a saint. She was a devout, churchgoing Episcopalian; in our house she knew Father gave the orders and she could only ask, so she asked all of us to go to church with her. Knowing the limits of her power, Bill and later Kirk begged off; knowing the limits of her power was probably the major reason I went with her.

She had a tyrant husband and, in some ways, three tyrannical sons; she had had a tyrant father and two tyrannical older brothers. She consoled herself as a child by learning, with her younger brother, to play the piano very well, and I have never seen anyone who seemed so happy to play. She loved to play while others sang, she seemed to know any song anyone else knew, and she could transpose it into any key. For years she played flute-piano duets with a man she did not much like, and grabbed any chance she could to play piano duets with our piano teacher. She would sing while washing dishes, and sing for what seemed like hours on long car trips. It is, thus, appropriate and wonderful that, in her seventies and beginning to lose touch with the world, she started singing a song to express her relation to all her male tyrants. She must have known it for years, but I had never heard her sing it. Its key lines are: "When he's sober he's an ogre, / When he's drunk he's just an ass; / And that's why I'm a grass widow, / With a sign saying 'Keep off the grass!' "

Mother had gone to Smith, and her younger brother, my name-sake, had gone to Yale, where he was the roommate of Jerome Hill, James J. Hill's grandson. As I reconstruct it, Helen and Roger Stearns and Romie Hill were for years the center of a group of people, most of whom were wealthy, read poetry, traveled, sang, and adored the theater. Roger was an actor and, later on, a cocktail pianist; Romie Hill made a book of photographs, an award-winning animated movie, and a documentary about Albert Schweitzer; Helen Stearns was a good and serious student, and after Smith she got an M.A. at Harvard and a Ph.D. at Yale, so that after weekends in New Haven or New York, or after a summer in Italy, she read literature and wrote a dissertation on Skelton. Theirs was a gay world when they were together (Roger and perhaps Romie too were gay sexually), light and bright and spark-ling, and when she married my father, Mother gave almost all of it up, as if conceding that its values were secondary and that she trusted herself only with a tyrant.

Upon the occasion of Father's death, and then again upon the occasion of Mother's, I wrote a note to an old friend of theirs, John Pope, whom they had known at Yale. I knew him only by Mother's report, and the report was that Father and Johnny Pope would sit up late on many nights, talking, being silent for long stretches, then talking some more. She conveyed to me that in those conversations, and perhaps especially in those long silences, was serious business, literary or language study that was beyond the likes of her and me, who were given to talkiness and to thinking that silent people were serious business. But when John Pope replied to my notes, each time it was not Father but Mother he wrote about, her laughter and charm, her giving him his first highball in London, 1927, before he knew Bill Sale or knew he was a fellow student of hers.

As a child, I knew Roger Stearns and Romie Hill as pure magic, partly because I saw them little; it was part of Mother's way of telling her life that she had, and knowingly, left behind her the life she led with them when she got married. Father, she would say, did not need money, and he, she would emphasize, would always know how to make a living and live up to his responsibilities. Father, she would say as if speaking high praise, never told her she smoked too much or wore too much lipstick. Father, I could see, indulged her the piano, the dinner parties, the friends with whom she laughed, his colleagues whom she charmed, the church where, I am sure, she prayed feelings she never spoke of. He would not indulge her the fact that she was smart, had as many degrees as he, or might want occasionally to speak as a separate person, but this I could not see.

Because she did not wish me to. In another family, a child can easily be torn when the parents are in thought and style so dissimilar, but Mother prevented such tearing by tolerating no conflict between herself and Father, or between his values and hers. She directed me to be in awe of Father's silence, never to see his orderliness as tyranny, and to value discipline more than warmth, laughter, or, in most senses of the term, love. With the buttress of her religious faith, she accepted her role cheerfully, and urged me to accept mine similarly. So we were good companions, but the message was that there were more important things than companionship. My mother's blessing is that while I could not emulate Father, while I was a second-class citizen, when I began to be free of my idolizing fear of Father, there was much my childhood with her had let me be, and become.

Until I was about ten, radio was more important than movies, and movies were more important than books. From ten until sixteen, movies were more important than either radio or books, though books were gaining in importance from twelve on and easily gained most of my attention after I went to college.

As a child, though I loved stories, I was seldom able to do more than dabble with books. The ones I remember most—the Oz books, Babar, the early Dr. Seuss, and Milne—were read to me between the ages of four and seven; after that, when I was expected to read on my own, I made little headway. I found it hard to imagine I would ever finish a book that had no pictures. I sometimes looked at page 100, or page 200, of a book and thought what an extraordinary person one must be to be able to read so many pages, and when I finally achieved that feat, with Louise Andrews Kent's *He Went with Marco Polo*, I was in the sixth grade and read as if losing my virginity, or crossing the bar. I have written elsewhere that "I was a daylight reader, seeking to live in a daylight world"; that is, I read to learn how to get along, to find out what I needed to know. What I wasn't, and could not dare even to wish to be though I knew him well, was Munro Leaf's Ferdinand the Bull. Ferdinand goes off by himself, shows himself immensely powerful when roused, and then refuses challenges offered to his power. Ferdinand fascinated and baffled me, but I could not even afford consciously to envy him, since to do so would tell me too much about who I was. I did better with Baum's Dorothy Gale, the great accepter and adapter, better than I was at these things, but like me.

Radio worked better. Afternoon serials, such as Jack Armstrong, I would listen to, but mostly when others my age were around. Early-evening comedy—Jack Benny, Phil Harris, Fred Allen—we listened to as a family, and their jokes amused Father and therefore amused me, because his humor was the only kind I understood. *Information Please* and *Quiz Kids* were just extensions of our dinner-table quizzes. Radio soap opera was a staple of summertime lunches, and they gave me a glimpse into the tangles of adult life, one that soon would be enlarged by the movies. From *Big Sister, Our Gal Sunday,* and *Helen Trent* I got a better sense of adults who were not my parents than I got from my friends' parents. What interested me was not so much the tangles, some of which I did not understand, but their openness, the frankness with which the disasters were faced, all of which was unknown in my family of unspoken treaties and demands. Helen Trent sought happiness "after thirty-five." Of course I didn't know what being over thirty-five meant, but I could be fascinated that one might seek happiness. So far as I knew, my world was innocent of such a search.

My childhood was really over by the time movies expanded the glimpses offered by the radio soaps. The movie fare of my childhood was essentially Saturday afternoon fare: Disney, *The Thief of Baghdad,* World War I movies such as *Sergeant York* and *The Fighting Sixty-Ninth,* Abbott and Costello comedies, Sabu-Maria Montez-Jon Hall exotica. I always had the feeling that others my age were allowed to go to the movies more often than I was, or could go at night long before I could, and most of my memories of movies are social experiences in which certain truths of dubious value were shared: movies without love stuff are good, Abbott and Costello are funny. The truth I never spoke was that I most loved the previews of movies I was not going to be allowed to see, and it is one sign that childhood was over when I could choose my own fare; it is another that at that point I went, or always wanted to go, alone, and to brood over such films as:

Watch on the Rhine, Scarlet Street, The Seventh Veil, The Woman in the Window, Davis, Stanwyck, Joan Bennett, and Baxter releasing longings in me as nothing in childhood had been able to do.

Very little, then, of popular culture made much difference to me until childhood was ending. Much the same is true of my relation to others my age, and their parents. Liking or disliking contemporaries did not enter clearly into my relation with boys my age; their proximity, availability, and willingness to accept me were what was important. Inevitably, I was more often with boys who played games, board games, sports, or toy soldiers, than with those who whittled, shot guns, did carpentry, or pursued other activities involving manual dexterity. We had spurts of games in which boys spaced some years apart could play, variations of hide-and-seek—Kick the Can, I Spy, Prisoner's Base—that I liked a lot because my relatively small size and foot speed made me a good player. But these are games for half a dozen and more players, and we seldom could get that many together, especially in the summer when the available mates shrank to the immediate neighborhood and we were lucky to get two or three together to do anything.

Recently a friend and I began a fascinating long conversation with his asking "Did you go home to other kids' houses when you were a child?" "Yes," was the answer, though not all that often; to be asked to stay for supper was even rarer, and for the night much rarer still. We tended to play softball or football on the school field more than visit each other's houses. There were, though, spurts when I would see a good deal of one boy or another for a little while, as though we were ransacking each other's houses to discover what we did not have at home, but these soon passed. I liked, when I was not intimidated, such things as reading comic books that were forbidden at home, or observing people do chores cooperatively, or seeing habits of messiness or neatness unknown at home. I was numbly fascinated by pets other than dogs, and by that strangest of creatures, sisters. But such pleasures as these tended to be overshadowed by the parents, especially the fathers. Danny Baxter's father told Danny and me "to get down off that balcony or I'll cut your ears off"; Bob Fay's father once made me turn around and go home, a mile's walk, because I'd phoned their house before 9 A.M.; Lin Webster's father sat in his study, wearing a green eyeshade, and doing nothing at all; Neil Baker's mother lived in rooms piled high with newspapers and shouted at her husband and children; Robin Palmer's father would come into a room where Robin and I would be playing chess or trying to get a baseball game on the radio, and he would stand, for five minutes maybe, asking us seriously to believe by his silence that nothing we were doing was ever worth doing. No wonder other boys came more often to the Sales', where we could play board games uninterruptedly in the basement and Mother was always friendly.

I have said that for Father in theory there was nothing not worth knowing, but in fact there was much he did not want to know and toward which he took a superior attitude that had a considerable effect on the way I saw what other children and adults did. Birds, for instance. Arthur Allen, a world-famous ornithologist, led some of our bird walks, and Father would not have dreamed of feeling superior to him. But amateurs who rose at what he thought an ungodly hour to look for birds, or who walked the neighborhood with binoculars around their necks, could be patronized as people only slightly above people who just took walks, which for him was the silliest thing one could do. Or cars. If any of his sons had gotten seriously interested in auto mechanics, that would have been fine, but an interest in cars, in makes, or speed, or performance, was vulgar. In his forty-five years in Ithaca, until just before he died, he owned four Buicks; he could say why, and why he took the car to Ned to have work done on it, but that was it. Or the *Syracuse Post-Standard,* a daily paper I saw in other people's houses but never in ours. Mother took and carefully read the *Ithaca Journal,* well and good. For years we got *PM,* the leftist New York newspaper, in the mail, and I learned about World War II from it, also well and good. Later we subscribed to the *New York Times,* well and good of course. Which left the *Syracuse Post-Standard,* a provincial, no-account newspaper, and one would no more have it around than send one's child to Syracuse University or go to Syracuse to shop. I doubt if Father was ever inside the Syracuse city limits, and he certainly did not think he would have to be in order to take the tone he did.

As I looked into the outside world, then, what did I see? Few birds smaller than a robin, as I have said, and I had no interest in cars, or Syracuse, but when I saw adults doing something not done in our house, or objects not to be found in ours, I would wonder if these were to be scorned, and later on I frequently was caught in the vise of simultaneously admiring and scorning. The question "What should I think?" was backed with the vague certainty that I should think something, take some attitude. I had friends, for instance, who had grandparents, aunts, uncles, and cousins living in or near Ithaca, and these families would meet on Sundays or holidays, for picnics, or fireworks, or Thanksgiving dinner. Father's parents lived in Louisville, and his sister died when I was young; of Mother's three brothers, none lived nearer than New York. What clues did I have about what attitude to take toward large family gatherings? Well, I enjoyed picnics, but knew that for Father they ranked alongside taking walks. Thanksgiving dinner, I was quite sure, Father put up with as a tiresome prelude to listening to the Cornell-Penn game. I envied people who had family gatherings, and minded when they made friends unavailable, yet I felt a tug that told me I should feel otherwise. The Fourth of July, thus, was desolate, because other families were doing things and we did nothing beyond hang out a large ancient American flag notable for having only forty-five stars. So too with birthday parties. Other boys had elaborate parties, and I loved going to them, yet the fact that Father seemed assiduously to avoid ours tugged me in another direction, from whence I could be tugged in yet another whenever my parents went to, or stranger still, gave, a birthday or anniversary party. Always there were so many things undiscussed that I had to read a great deal out of things said indirectly, out of silences, yet having to do that seemed to insulate me from people outside the family, especially people I knew my parents knew only distantly. I was, thus, easily shocked when I heard something, such as swearing, in another house that I never heard in ours, and was baffled and intrigued, as I was with the radio soaps, when family tangles or quarrels were spoken of at all. I probably was fortunate that though other people clearly did or said things I was attracted to, there was no boy, no parent, out there who clearly offered promises of life that I did not know at home. Had there been, I could only have begun rebelling and longing before I had equipment or ammunition enough.

No wonder, then, that food was a great mystery. Father had close to the narrowest possible taste in foods—and, of course, everyone's tastes were narrowed during the war. He had, to be sure, definite ideas on how well done meat should be cooked, and he knew the only way to cook an egg (boiled, four minutes), and why it was that the onions, garlic, herbs, and spices the world has used for millennia should be used sparingly or, preferably, not at all. Of starches, one ate potatoes often, rice seldom, and pasta never. Of vegetables, only beans, lima beans, carrots, peas, and corn in summer; Mother would cook herself cabbage, broccoli, or sprouts, but since Father did not touch them, we did not eat them either. Of meats, beef, lamb, chicken, pork rarely, and fish on Friday, and terrible bony fish it was too. It would surprise no one that I never saw a shellfish until I was twenty, but that I saw my first pork chop at fifteen, or my first fried egg when I went to college?

What to make, then, of food offered me in other people's houses, or in restaurants? It wasn't that I was suddenly faced with anything more exotic than lasagna or stewed celery. But we did not have butter at home, and I knew that bread or rolls with butter that I ate outside our house were much better than those with margarine at home, and I once ate a quarter pound of butter by itself in a house where I was baby-sitting. Chili was unknown at home—it had spiciness as well as the wrong kind of beans—and if I didn't care for the beans, I loved the hotness, though I was afraid to love it and, especially, to admit it. Father would not tolerate really rare meat, and I remember little of it in other people's homes, but rare hamburger tasted unaccountably good, and my first prime rib in a restaurant, when I was an adolescent, hinted to me as strongly as did my favorite movies that there were things to long for in the world outside. Small things at friends' homes—soup as a first course, water glasses, people able to serve themselves, ice cream for a snack—could dazzle me. Yet always there was the tug. Father was right, surely, and therefore my tastes when they differed from his had to be puzzling to me. Much as I loved butter, the imprisoning grip of childhood was so strong that when we were first married I told my wife that margarine was preferable.

One reason margarine was preferable is that it is cheaper, which brings me to money, a mystery even greater than food, the only one of the great mysteries I knew much about as a child. I placed much of my sense of the mysterious onto money. Of sex I knew less than most children, because I had no sisters, because Mother talked little about herself as a woman and Father never mentioned it, and because we were not encouraged to ask questions that had no definite answers. I knew nothing mysterious about religion; it was what I did on Sunday mornings. Of death I knew nothing until a dog of ours, and then a neighbor, died when I was twelve. So money was the great mystery, both because its effects could be felt everywhere and because it was almost never mentioned.

Born in 1932, I did not learn of the Depression until it was almost over, and was never directly affected by it. Mother married Father before the Crash, though her family had lost much of its money before that, and she had reason to say he would always be able to earn a living, as many she knew before meeting him could not. He was making $1,800 as an instructor at Yale the year I was born, and came to Cornell in 1936 at $3,600, perfectly adequate salaries. Mother had some stocks, and I remember checks from Marine Midland or American Radiator appearing in the mail periodically. Of other details, of how much anything cost, I knew little and can reconstruct little now, though I know Father's salary went up little in the decade after 1936, and that after his sister died he fully supported his parents and a cousin.

There was no poverty and no threat of poverty. 309 The Parkway is a nice house and has, as I have said, a large lot. Buicks are Buicks. The fear of extravagance or expense which pervaded our house was as much a matter of style as of necessity, though I did not know that. But I know that when, in 1940, we were to visit New York, to see the World's Fair and stay with Romie Hill, Bill and I got new clothes, matching T-shirts, shorts for me, and long trousers for Bill, and that is my only recollection in the middle years of childhood of when I wore clothes bought for me. Everything else, except for shoes, was handed down. This does not mean I was dressed badly, but it does mean I had no choices and that I must not ask. It is the Do Not Ask that needs stressing.

I was not conscious of clothes until high school, though the boy who cannot tie his shoes or button his fly must present something of a spectacle, and I was aware of that. I am conscious, however, of feeling that when it came to baseball mitts, or bicycles, or ice skates, or, a little later, of money to spend on a movie or an ice-cream cone, that I must not ask. Since I am left-handed and no one else I knew was, I wore right-handed mitts or none at all until I was twelve, when a friend of a friend sold me, of all things, a left-handed catcher's mitt, the only one I've ever seen. I did not learn to ride a bike until after everyone else because there was no bike for me to ride until I was eight or nine and I inherited one from Bill. When others had hockey skates I was still wearing heirloom figure skates. For years I heard of others my age having an allowance, but I had only what I earned, probably until high school.

There is nothing terribly restrictive about all this. The inherited bike and ice skates were perfectly serviceable, and baseball mitts fit more easily on either hand then than did the models developed after the war. If others had allowances, or went more often to the movies, the nearest place to buy ice cream was two miles away, and the nearest movie was three, too far to get to easily or often until childhood was almost over. Nonetheless I knew that others had things that I wanted and that not even Father would scorn, and I did not know why this was so and I did know I could not ask, either for the things or for the reason. If this mattered little at age six or seven, it mattered increasingly thereafter.

I had no choice but to assume that we were not poor but were poorer than others, that I was poorer than my brother Bill, and that this defined something like a fate. This fate, when fitted with my being a year younger in school, impressively clumsy, a loser in most games, the only one in school who wore glasses, a quick wit where quick wits are imperative but hard wits are better, comes close to feeling like a personal identity. It did much to isolate me, even from my brothers, who shared much of my culture and fate. Mother was the only person whose love I knew, and whom I knew I loved, but she would never talk about money, and would only urge me to accept other aspects of my fate or identity.

I had two weapons against whatever feelings all this yielded. I could accept cheerfully, as Mother urged, or I could try to scorn what I did not have, as I suspected Father would have done. My attempts at scorn were pitiful, but I learned very young how to employ cheerfulness as a way of burying wants and turning away wrath. Not all these wants had to do with money, but since many of the nonfinancial aspects of the fate were constants and did have to be accepted, the desire for things that could be bought could fluctuate, and often grew strong enough to become a real test of my ability to be cheerful. Of course one was left-handed, but did that mean one was never to have a left-handed mitt? Was it wrong to want one? I was much more conscious of wanting things than anyone knew I was.

It did not help that in Cayuga Heights there were people of real wealth, people with maids, friends who always had their own bedrooms, or wrist watches, or elegant pocket knives. Nor did it help that Mother cheerfully got along with whatever she had and that Father seemed to scorn what he did not have. Nor did it help, finally, that I acted poorly with whatever money I did have. "Save up your money" is the financial equivalent of "Whatever you work at, really work," and I heard, and failed, both messages often. I had dimes, and some quarters, so I could of course have saved them into enough dollars to buy that left-handed mitt, but that would take months, and the lad with the short attention span would spend the money long before it was saved and then act cheerful, as though he could do as well without. I could then doubly envy a friend who not only had a wrist watch but had saved in order to get it, and feel doubly ashamed for feeling the envy.

Scorning the possession of something you really want is a kind of lying, and so too can cheerfulness become when employed as I often employed it. My childhood began to end when I began to feel myself unhappy, to employ lying as a kind of power, as when I plagiarized three Ogden Nash poems in the eighth grade, and to become the financial equivalent of a liar, namely, a thief. To feel and do these things was only to deepen and hasten the self-ostracization that probably would have come anyway. I began to go to the movies by myself, to walk or ride my paper route with lonely cheerfulness and my dog, to brood about girls, to see the boys I had gone through grade school with as little as possible, and to feel a strong need for friendship and real conversation. In other words, to become adolescent.

On the edge of that frontier I read Betty Smith's *A Tree Grows in*

Brooklyn, my first adult book. I was twelve, in the eighth grade. I read it feverishly, then reread it many times in the next few years; when I reread it recently, it effortlessly caught me in its grip all over again. I was once asked to give a talk about my favorite book, and I began a history of such books with Betty Smith's. Afterward a young woman, clearly perplexed, asked how it was possible that my favorite book could have been what for her clearly was a girl's book. Therein lies the tale; it was so compelling because it told of a world of which I knew nothing.

There was, first, not the nameless and unreal genteel poverty of my childhood, but rigorous poverty that could be spoken of in dollars and cents, could be shared, could yield small treats on important days. It did no harm that Smith's nostalgic retrospect softens some of the blows of what it must have been like day by day, especially for the mother. I cannot say I then wanted to be poor, but I did envy the sense of sharing that it yielded, and the strong sense of details—objects, smells, holidays—that accompanied it and that my life lacked. Chores and work created a feeling of accomplishment, of contributing to a family, that my work never had.

There was, second, Johnny Nolan's alcoholism, important for itself and for what it meant to the family. Once one of the children is sent to fetch Johnny from McGarrity's saloon, where he "had settled down to an afternoon of serious drinking." What did it mean to be able to do that? The only thing the adults I knew settled into seriously for an afternoon was reading, or the Metropolitan Opera. Of drink itself I knew next to nothing, did not even know of my parents' great fear of drinking, and had never seen anyone drunk. So it felt like an alternative way of life, not attractive in itself, but something the knowledge of which had been kept from me. Johnny's alcoholism did not, furthermore, turn him into a monster. Francie went on loving him and needing his love, and his alcoholism even helped clarify for her what it meant to a child to love a parent as opposed to needing one or obeying one. Much as I loved my mother, I had no such weakness in a parent that might help create such clarity.

Third, here was Katie, the linchpin of the family in a way I knew no woman to be, and her sister Sissie, whose frank sexuality I knew nothing of, certainly not in a woman. My world was so strictly patriarchal that I had to believe patriarchy was nature-made or God-given. But here was Katie, acting not out of choice but with a strength my mother would die rather than admit she had or needed; trying to live with a drunk husband she pities as well as loves; making plans and making sure they are kept; telling Francie and Neely what those plans are. I could take in Sissie's sexuality only with other things about her new to me—her marriages and her stillborn babies—and place them all at a distance, as part of city or immigrant life. The scene in which Sissie gives Johnny a drink and gets him to fall asleep between her breasts I stared at as I might now stare at a piece of Aztec sculpture; if that was possible, how very little I knew of life, and how little those around me were going to be able to tell me.

There was, finally and most important, Francie. I had no sisters and our immediate neighborhood had no girls remotely my age. By custom girls did not play with boys at recess or after school, and by custom girls had that neat handwriting that seemed the key to good grades. The only girl I knew well was Baum's Dorothy Gale, but her likeness to me in other ways led me to ignore our sexual difference. It seems literally true that after playing doctor with Barbara Shirey when I was four and she was three I never did anything with a girl and saw girls as if looking through the long end of a telescope. If someone said there were girls I went through nine years of grade school with and never spoke to, I could not deny it. Martha Kelsey, Anne Cottrell, Margaret Morris, Deborahs Williams, Knott, and Cornell, Mari Hartell, Helen Kiely—I might as well be naming first-magnitude stars, or cities in France. There had been a slight change in the seventh grade when, for one year only, my and everyone's life was brightened by Mary Harris, who laughed openly, who played games with boys as well as girls, and with whom I talked as seriously as I had ever talked to anyone except my mother. Even Mary, though, could tell me little about what it was like to be her, or a girl.

Francie Nolan could, or could begin to. She showed me that we shared many thoughts and feelings despite her being a girl, poor, and the daughter of a drunk in Brooklyn in 1912. She sought, for instance, and failed to get the same approval from her mother that I sought and failed to get from my father. Sister and brother for her resembled brother and brother for me, shared experiences rather than open loving when young, drifting apart when older. That girls and women were, like me, people, was not a lesson I could learn from one book at age twelve, but I could start. All the more reason, thus, to be fascinated, dismayed, and frightened, and almost precisely to the same extent that Francie is, when she has her first menstrual period; no one had told either of us about that. That nothing happens to her immediately after that, no romance or sexual experience, was also compelling because it meant that there were things of the flesh that were not things of the heart, and both Francie and I were going to have to live with that fact.

A Tree Grows in Brooklyn, then, was *life,* not a trip to Oz or Pooh Corner, and beginning to feel all that I was ignorant of, all that had been kept from me by people and circumstance, I was fortunate in being able to share so much with Francie Nolan and thereby begin to grope toward my life. It should come as no surprise that the next book that mattered to me as this one did was Lawrence's *Sons and Lovers*.

Up until age twelve, then, my culture was family culture, though the family itself was never closely knit. It was because my parents, as well as being my parents, were, in different ways, powerful and interesting people. It was because Cayuga Heights was all nuclear families that showed little of divorced or single people, the elderly, or childless couples. It was because commerce was removed and the cultural pulls and sense of differences offered by city life were unknown. It was because my school was just across the street and its values never clashed with family values. Life moved out away from my family like concentric circles made by a stone dropped on a still pond. If I often was baffled by what I saw outside my home, and if there were things out there I wanted, I was not compelled even in feeling to try to move toward them. There was certainly no other family I wanted to be part of, and no adult I liked as much as my mother.

Childhood begins to end when the outside world really begins to beckon and to pull, when I began to feel my ignorance and therefore the limits of my family's knowledge and way of life. I made a trip to Cleveland at the end of the war and stayed with my uncle's family, a very different one from ours, and saw major-league baseball, ate rich foods, and was, for the first time, propositioned by a homosexual. I went to high school and saw beautiful girls and rough lads from the parochial school and the farms. I went to the movies as often as I could afford. I began to hunger for the life out there, in almost any form it took. Though no girl or woman could love me, I could long to fall hopelessly in love, like a character in a movie or a popular song. Since I could not join the world out there, I was alone, but even the misery of that aloneness was a different feeling from what I had known as a child.

One afternoon, during the summer before I turned thirteen and went to high school, I was sitting on the porch with Mother. I have no idea of what we were talking about, but at one moment she said, not looking at me but not self-consciously turning away either, "Everyone has a dirty mind." A perfect gift with which to usher a son out of his childhood. No one better to tell me this, since no one was less likely to, at least in the life I thus, and then, was leaving.

Index